I PASS AS
WHITE

William "Tex" Pointer

NEWMAN SPRINGS PUBLISHING
320 Broad Street
Red Bank, NJ 07701

First originally published by Newman Springs Publishing 2021

ISBN 978-1-63881-320-0 (Paperback)
ISBN 978-1-63881-321-7 (Digital)

Printed in the United States of America

To Jum and Francis, two wonderful people whose love and understanding I shall always cherish

Acknowledgments

I would like to thank and give credit to *Collier's Magazine* for permission to use one of its editorials, "A Challenge to Bigotry," and to Mr. George E. Sokolsky of the Kings Features Syndicate to use excerpts from his article "South Pacific."

The Author

Introduction

I am sitting here now running the past back before the present, some good and some bad, yet I wouldn't have missed any of it.

I once read that a home is never vacant—it lives with the memory of the past—and that life itself exists in history. Vacant halls echo the resounding of feet long since dead that lived, loved, and fought there; and as such, a story has no ending. It is only a link between the past and the future, a never-ending search for something we know not what.

This has been my life—looking blindly, supposedly for happiness, and running from the past only to discover more unrest, sorrow, and then eventually happiness and contentment.

To begin with, I am no writer. I can never see myself as a great author, but I can put down on paper facts and actual events that I hope will shock you. They are all real, very real, and took place somewhere within these great forty-eight states of ours.

I have lived in misery and felt pain and heartaches, but what one of us hasn't? Yes. I have felt pain and misery. But why? That's the point we completely overlook—why?

I'll tell you why—ignorance and a small-minded world.

Ignorance—the greatest sin in the world and a compassionate one, the thing that makes men forget that they are men and the thing that makes nations start wars that soon envelop the world, bringing nothing but sorrow and chaos in the end. It not only made my life a "living hell." It can make it so for every human being all over the universe.

I have tried to tell my story, my life story, in a way that everyone can understand what hate, poverty, and ignorance can do to a nation. This is my life—a story of a boy, a man, in this great country of America with the ambition and ideals to get ahead. In these pages, you will see the price I paid to get security, freedom, and happiness for me and my family.

I

Like most children, my early life was normal and of little interest. I was born in a small southwestern town in Texas that since has grown into a thriving metropolis for my parents. They were the best and still are, both being alive at this moment.

There was always the best they could afford for me, which was better than the average. As a child, an abundance of toys; as a growing boy, clothes, enjoyment, and love; and as a young man, a good education. Things would have been so different if I had what Mom wanted, a college education and a lawyer's degree, but our children come from us, not of us. They may have the same color of skin as us, or eyes that match ours or certain features, but they have not our minds or brains. Their thoughts are their own to do with as they see fit, and so as it was with me.

At school, I had always been an A pupil, with an occasional C in deportment; but due to a hotheaded, childish stunt during summer vacation before my last semester of high school, I resolved I didn't want college. As a matter of fact, I didn't want anything that had any connection or ties with my hometown.

It was one of those hot, sultry July mornings that Texas is known for, the kind that we brag about and tell you how an egg will fry on the sidewalk. Our house sits back about twenty-five feet from the street bordered with evergreen hedges and a lawn that stretches to the curb. Between the sidewalk and driveway, there are two large hackberry trees where one could always find my father reading after dinner (but in the morning, it was the neighborhood kids' hangout). This particular morning, there were about eight of us sprawled there beneath the trees, fixing bicycles or just plain loafing. Mom and Dad were both at work, and only my kid sister was in the house. As always, there must be a neighborhood bully, and this day found him in my yard. Walter was all right; it was just that being a preacher's son, he had been spoiled.

My idea of a perfect description is a fat slob of seventeen weighing about 160 pounds and completely lazy. By comparison of size, I was only a dwarf; but in brains, I had him licked. At that time, I was a tall, scrawny beanpole weighing 125 and had always given him a wide berth. It wasn't fear of him that made me do this as much as what his father stood for in the community. As silly as it seems, a young boy of sixteen sees things through strange eyes, and you don't know what a big preacher in a small town can do. At any rate, I had never had trouble with him; but on this day, he was itching to start it like a horse chafing at the bit.

Having picked on everyone without successfully starting a fight, he was reluctantly giving up when my kid sister came out of the house. I say my sister because she has never been regarded in any way but as such although in reality she is adopted. From the first day she came to live with us, she has been loved as a sister. Julie was eight years old at the time and just recovering from illness. Upon seeing her, Walter started meddling with renewed vigor; only now, it was directed solely at Sis. I would have overlooked the whole thing if he hadn't grabbed her arm.

As she has taken shots for the past three months, her arm was naturally sore, and she started crying. He persisted in pulling her by this arm. Until now, all the fellows were watching me for some signs of rescue. Without moving from the lawn, I told him to turn her loose and that I thought it would be best if he went home.

That was all he wanted. I had played right into his hands.

He released Julie and slowly turned on me.

With sly smiling face and hands on hips, he remarked, "I don't think you can make me go home, and I don't like to leave a place until I'm good and ready."

There was no use my lying on the ground arguing, not with him standing there looking for an excuse to pounce on me.

Rising to my feet, I took Julie by the hand, saying, "Come, Sis. We'll go in the house until he leaves."

I expected him to grab me any minute, and when he made no move to do so, I started around him for the porch. The fellows had not moved since Julie entered the yard, and now all eyes were following me. One of the gangs sitting near the steps was using a knife to pick a valve stem from an inner tube. As I passed him and started up the steps, there was a scuffling movement behind me.

Turning, I was confronted with Walter standing in an arrogant, cocksure manner brandishing the knife.

I saw at a glance what had happened. He had simply jerked the knife from the boy's hand, and he was now repeating his first remark, "I'll go home when I please." I could have stood for anything except his repeating this last phrase again. As I saw him standing there with such childish bravado in front of the fellows, something just snapped inside me. It's funny how we remember small happenings, but one strange thing has always remained with me. Rushing into the house, taking Julie with me, I went straight to my parents' bedroom and, throwing back the pillow, found what I wanted—my father's .45 revolver. I kissed Sis; and upon reaching the porch, for no apparent reason, I turned and locked the door. I have always wondered why; at any rate, it doesn't matter now.

I knew exactly what I was going to do, and I was mad enough to carry it out. When I told Walter to leave the yard, I meant it. He was still standing at the foot of the steps, and in my turning to lock the door, the gun had not been seen. As I turned to face him, bringing the gun up, everyone was frozen with fear including Walter; but in the next second, all hell broke loose. The kids dived for cover, and he made a dive for the corner of the house. I was right on his heels, but when I reached the corner, he was dodging between cars and disappearing rapidly up the street.

Here began my mistake, my hotheaded error, my close brush with the law. Not being satisfied with removing him from the yard, I now set out to do a good job of removal. Knowing he might expect me to follow, I decided to cut through the alley coming out directly in front of his home. The neighborhood was not alarmed or disturbed yet because only the fellows saw what happened, and I guess they were still running. Being careful to keep the gun concealed in case I ran into anyone, I finally reached a large tree directly across the street from him. He must have expected me to follow, for he was standing there looking in the direction from which he had just come. I was both satisfied and happy. I had fooled him. As for handling the gun, that was a cinch. My father was a great one for hunting, and from the time I was old enough, I had been taught how to handle practically every make of firearm. For a moment, I just stood there watching him, thinking how much I hated his kind and all that he stood for. True, we were only kids—he's seventeen and I'm sixteen—but sometimes, as I said before, it's surprising what goes on in a kid's mind. Raising the gun, I took careful aim, and then I called to him. At the sound of my voice, he whirled to face me; but only for a moment because, in the next second, he was half running and half stumbling toward the house. As he reached the porch, I fired.

I thank God now that I missed although at the time I wanted to kill him in the worst way. Luckily, due to my temper, I had forgotten the one important thing—the kick of the gun. That's what saved him and me. The gun was aimed at his back, and when I fired at that distance, the kick-up caused both bullets to miss his head by inches. Had I aimed at his waist, he would have been hit both times, squarely in the back. The police later found the bullets in the door facing just above where he entered, which meant that I only missed by about eight inches—a close but lucky margin to have a man's death off my hands.

Doors opened; windows were raised. Suddenly the street was alive with wondering faces and questioning voices. Everyone had heard, but no one had seen. So I calmly turned and walked down the alley toward home.

In five minutes, I was sitting on the porch as if nothing had happened. The gun was reloaded, empty shells thrown away, and the bed made. I knew the police were coming. I could see the neighbors standing down the street all looking at me; and then squad car number 8 turned the corner, drove to the house, and stopped. Walter was in the back seat with Craig, the officer, trying to quiet him long enough to find out what had happened. Vincent, the wise cop driving, got out and came after me.

"Where is the gun?" he asked.

With childish ignorance, I gave him the simple lie that my father had been home eating lunch when I returned and had taken the gun back to work with him. This, as I should have known, didn't satisfy him; and he told me so in no uncertain words. I was ordered into the house with him following close behind. The first thing he did was to pull out a vanity drawer, but he made no effort to hold it. He just dropped it and let the contents go everywhere.

I had heard of cops wrecking a place, and it was plain that he intended doing just that. So I got the gun. That's all he wanted, and upon receiving it, he marched me out to the front seat of the cruiser, and off we went to headquarters at the city hall. I will admit I was pretty scared by now and trembling more every minute. When we reached the city hall, I was placed in what they call the bullpen. I was getting more worried as the minutes went by, mainly because they hadn't asked me any questions, not one, about the shooting.

Then it began, a regular procession of curious faces and a muffled whispered conversation, and I didn't need to guess what it was about. I knew. I had faced it before, and now I had the feeling of a caged wild animal or a freak that was on exhibition to a snickering, whispering public. Through the small barred window in the door, I could see the faces that belied their look of casual interest as though it was a natural act to look in at me. There was the desk sergeant's wife who had come down to pick him up as he went off duty. She had no right or reason to be outside my cell back here in a jail corridor, but she was there nevertheless, looking and snickering in disbelief. There were others, many others after her. They all came for the same reason, and I could do nothing.

Was I to be confronted always with repetition of things like this—a gossipy word, a half-hidden laugh, and a constant reminder that I was different from them? It wasn't my fault. I had been born this way, and there was nothing anyone could do about it. Why did they do these things? There was nothing physically or mentally wrong with me, and everyone said I was good-looking, especially with this mop of curly black hair. Then why? What made them persecute me in this manner? I could find no answer, and I knew it. This was an old argument with my inner self, and I knew that it had me licked. So I resigned myself to the inevitable fate that I could do nothing to stop it. With this false consolation in mind, I lay down to try to forget, to escape from my own thoughts in sleep. There was no sleep, no rest from prying eyes, and no escape from my tortured mind for nearly two hours; and relief was known only when the turnkey on duty opened the door and told me I was being taken to the juvenile office at the court house.

I had no time for thought now because once at the juvenile office, they really opened up with questions—who I was, what happened, why I did it, and so on—for about a half hour. By now, I didn't mind so much due to the fact that Mr. Brown, the juvenile officer, had a way of making you feel at ease as though he understood. After holding a job like that for a while, I guess it became natural to know how to handle kids like Walter and me. Speaking of Walter, I hadn't seen him since we arrived at city hall. I later found out that he had been released at once, mainly because he was the preacher's son.

"Oh well."

Mr. Brown, after he had finished questioning me, said he would have to hold me until my parents came. That meant he wasn't able to get in touch with them, and I would have to remain there until they came home and found out for themselves.

Well, I waited, and about three o'clock, Mom came in. When my mom arrived home from work, the neighbors had wasted no time giving her the "wonderful news." At any rate, I was really glad to see her.

After introductions between her and Mr. Brown, they began to discuss me. Mom was plainly shaken and couldn't understand what had possessed me to do such a thing. Mr. Brown had the floor for the next fifteen minutes, starting by explaining his position and ending by telling Mom I was free to go home with her but I would be tried at a closed hearing before a judge Friday morning at nine o'clock. Today was Tuesday.

I went home truthfully expecting to get a good shellacking which I deserved, and there was a dreaded fear of meeting Dad. My father is a very understanding man and always believed in speaking to me as man to man, but for this, I didn't believe he would be in a talking mood. When we arrived home, Dad was there, and he had already heard about it. He kissed Mom, spoke to me, and went right on reading the evening newspaper. That really hurt. He was giving me the silent routine, and he kept it up until after supper. It was then he came out on the porch and told me he wanted to, as he put it, discuss this unheard-of incident. We talked for about thirty minutes with me doing more listening than talking. The main topic was that our family had never been in trouble with the law, that it was a sinful wrong to take upon myself the responsibility of another man's life, and, last, that he never wanted my mother hurt as she had been today. If God was willing and I got out of this, he asked my promise that I would always walk a straight line. I gave my promise with sincerity, and I am truthfully sorry that I broke it. It was the only promise I ever broke to my father. Whether it was fate or my way of life, the promise was broken because I have had to fight every way, good or bad, for my chance at life, success, and freedom.

As sure as the sun must rise, Friday came, and nine o'clock found Dad and me in court. Walter and the pastor were already there, both looking as if they owned the world. The judge entered and immediately opened the case. Naturally both sides were to be heard, and Walter was called on first. By the time he had finished telling his story and I was called, fear had begun to take over. I stood up, faced the judge, and told him everything just as it had happened, omitting and adding nothing. When I finished, I just stood there watching him, hanging on to his every breath and his every facial expression.

It seemed an eternity before he spoke, and when he did, I wasn't prepared for his question. I was pinned to the spot when in a very blunt and direct manner he asked, "Are you sorry?" This had me; I couldn't answer. I wasn't raised that way. I've always placed soul satisfaction above everything else, and I knew if I answered him truthfully from the heart, I would make it tougher for myself because I wasn't sorry. I was still mad enough even then to tear Walter apart before his eyes. No, I knew I couldn't say that to him. I knew I had to lie, to humble myself for the sake of pity, and to say I was sorry. Then it dawned on me if I did this, I would hate myself; and without further hesitation, I answered, "It wasn't right. That I won't deny, but under the circumstances, if I found myself in the same position again, I would do it all over without regret." There was an immediate murmur in the back of me from everyone in the room, and looking at Dad, I could see he was stunned by what I had said. Upon hearing this surprising answer from me, the judge bowed his head as if in deep thought. Looking up, he beckoned the court recorder; and after a quick whispered conversation between the two, Walter and I were asked to step forward.

We stood there facing him, standing side by side while he went through the legal procedure of his findings—a strong and loud lecture on law and right and wrong, his personal opinion, and finally the punishment or sentence.

Looking from one to the other of us, he said, "I find you both guilty and sentence you both to two years"—here, he paused, and I nearly dropped before he continued—"but in view of certain aspects of the case, I suspend sentence and place you both on probation for two years. You will report to Mr. Brown in his office the tenth of each month."

When we left court, I could see that Dad was pretty mad, but all he said was "That damn soul satisfaction, as you call it, will get you killed someday." Walter had received the same sentence, and for that, I felt good, even happy. At least Mr. Brown had not placed the blame on me alone.

Within a week, I guess, the whole thing had quieted down; but I had made up my mind about the future. Upon finishing high school, I planned to leave home. I didn't know where I would go, but I had given Oklahoma City a lot of thought. Nothing was said to the family until after graduation, and then the argument started. Mom would hear no part of it, but Dad was very understanding. He finally convinced her that it might be the best thing for me and, as he put it, it would do me a world of good to get out on my own. As far as my probation was concerned, it wasn't hard for Dad to get Mr. Brown to agree to my going away as long as I was going to live with an aunt in Oklahoma City who didn't exist. Well, that's the way it all started. I was on my own to face the world. I graduated in February, and by May, I was on my way to Oklahoma City, Oklahoma.

Earlier this year, I read in The Cincinnati Enquirer of a celebration in honor of Robert Frost, America's most distinguished living poet and four-time Pulitzer Prize winner.

All day long, he had been answering questions, and finally this question was put to him: "In all your years and all your travels, what do you think is the most important thing you've learned about life?"

He paused a moment and then replied:

> In three words, I can sum up everything I've learned about life: It goes on. In all the confusions of today with all our troubles, with politicians and people slinging the word *fear* around, all of us become discouraged, tempted to say this is the end, the finish of life but it goes on. It always has, it always will. Just a little while back, at my farm near Ripton, Vermont, I planted a few more trees. You wonder why?

> Well, I'm like the Chinese of ninety who did the same thing. When they asked him why, he said that the world wasn't a desert when he came into it and wouldn't be when he departed. Those trees will keep on growing after I'm gone and after you're gone. I don't hold with people who say "Where do we go from here?" or "What's the use?" I wouldn't get up in the morning if I thought we didn't have a direction to go in. But if you ask me what the direction is, I can't answer.

> It's different for each of us. The important thing to remember is that there is a direction and a continuity even if so often we think we're lost. Despite our fears and our worries, and they're very real to all of us, life continues... It goes on.

These three words above all else in my eighty
years I've learned. (The Cincinnati Enquirer,
September 5, 1954)

And so it was with me. Life continued.

II

Oklahoma City is the capital of Oklahoma, seat of Oklahoma County, and largest city in the state on the northern branch of the Canadian River and in the center of the state. Great natural gas and oil fields are nearby with the state capital having oil wells on its lawn.

The site was opened to settlement in 1889. The city became the state capital in 1911, and it is indeed a beautiful place.

I arrived in Oklahoma City in the morning about ten o'clock and, by three o'clock, had a job. It wasn't much, but it was a start—dishwasher at $8 and meals per week. I knew there were better jobs around, but this one would carry me until I landed one. After two weeks had passed, I still hadn't found one. Good jobs were plentiful enough, but they were always taken or "We'll let you know," where I was concerned. I would apply for a job, and the interview would be all in my favor until one thing was mentioned. It was the same old story, my difference from everyone else. I was debating this problem about a week later in the café. Dawn was just breaking, and in a while, the streets would slowly start to fill with the rush of early morning workers. As the sun began to rise, you could see that it was going to be a beautiful day; and for some reason, I was glad. I suddenly remembered another sunrise, another day, a long time ago.

I had always visited my grandparents on the farm during my summer vacation. There was no doubt of my love for the country, the out-of-door life, and when I came, I usually stayed all summer vacation from school. It was on a day just like this. I would be turning fourteen next month, and for my birthday, I was returning home to have a big party. I had already visited with Mama Mary and Papa

Jim for almost two months; and I would be glad to get home to Mom and Dad although there was never loneliness for me on the farm because I always had hunting, fishing, the horses, Snookum the house dog, and Louise. I had played with Louise as long as I could remember. Even before we had sold our farm and moved to the city, I was aware that it would always be just playmates and nothing more. Her parents, Mr. and Mrs. Kiles, lived in the big house up at the corner. Mr. Kiles wasn't rich, but he was well-off and owned the biggest house and the best equipment of any farm for miles around. On this morning, Mama Mary had sent me with setting eggs for Mrs. Kiles's hens; and as I trudged along with Snookum, I was planning what Louise and I would do today.

As I reached the house, Louise came running out to meet me, and we went into the kitchen together. Mrs. Kiles was there, and after taking the eggs, she sat me down to a big glass of cold milk and sugar cookies. She asked me how Mama Mary was and if Papa Jim was through haying yet when I was going home and a lot of other things that I half heard. I was hurrying my milk and cookies so that Louise and I could get down to the creek. Suddenly I was aware that Mrs. Kiles had quit talking to me when I heard Louise ask her why she couldn't go out to play. Without answering, she went into the next room, calling Louise after her. I wasn't eavesdropping but couldn't help overhearing Mrs. Kiles as she tried to explain to her.

"There are some things you are too young to understand. But you are thirteen years old, and it's not right for you to play with William so much now. You and William are different, Louise, and well, we just don't do things like that down here. I know he's a good boy, but you will have to stop playing with him from now on. As I said before, you and William are different. Why, even your religion is different, and after all, this is Texas."

I didn't wait to hear any more. I just picked up my cap and quietly left. I had heard it all before, many times before. I knew what it was about—this "William's different." It wasn't the first time. I could walk down the street and see two people whispering with one pointing at me, both looking in an awestruck manner, a look of wonder and disbelief. I knew what they said and wondered even though they were too cowardly to say it openly. This never bothered me. Never. It was always why. That was my worry—why?

Why was the public like this? Why had Mrs. Kiles planted that same root in Louise's mind, a clean and unprejudiced mind? This word *different*—why was I different? I knew what *different* meant concerning me, but why did it have to be that way? Physically we were the same other than sex. Both our complexions were White. Our eyes were the same color and hair of same texture, except mine was dark and curly. Both our minds had been clean and good until just now when her own mother had placed the seed that eventually grew into hate and intolerance. Why should a mother commit such a sin as this on her own daughter, because that's exactly what you would call it, "a sin". Speaking of sin, what had Mrs. Kiles meant by "Why, even your religions are different"? There was a difference; but even I, a kid of fourteen, knew there was no difference basically. She was a Catholic, and I was Baptist. So what did she mean by her remark? Was she stupid enough to really believe that there were five or six Gods in heaven, one for every religion?

When my Dad explained it to me, he just said, "We all worship, pray, and give penance in a different way, but basically it's all the same to God. In the end, there is no difference. Heaven is such that all who have lived well, of whatever race or religion, have a place there." I had fought this argument before, and I was right back to the same place. Why? Why was it like this? Why did the public, the world, let it go on this way? It was too much for me to analyze, and I knew as before that it had me licked. That summer, I went back to the city and home, and even though I have visited my grandparents many times since, I have never spent an entire summer vacation there.

Strange that this beautiful sunrise here in Oklahoma City, so far from Texas, should take me back ten many years in the past. Maybe it was my present condition, this new fight with my old adversary. I say old because I had fought with him many times before. I fought him as a child and then through elementary and high school, and from all outlooks, I would fight him through all the days of my life. Why must it be this way? Why did the world let a condition of this type exist? Did we all express outside that we were against prejudice, hate, and intolerance yet inside, deep, deep down inside, we all feel a malicious lust for conditions of this type? I couldn't bring myself to believe this because if it were true, then we, every one of us in America, were destroying the great principles that have been built since our forefathers drew the plans for the Constitution of the United States. But if this were so, we would be back in less than a hundred years to the days of lords and peasants, where the rich can't be bothered with the poor, where the lord is master and the peasant is slave, and where the courts are disinterested in the criminal other than to convict. Last but most important, there would be one religion and one government forced on the world. So, you see, no one has the right to say "It's not my problem. Let someone else solve it." Each one of us has the responsibility of worrying, as we call it, over the problems of our fellow man. Remember the old biblical question, "Am I my brother's keeper?" The answer is "Yes, we all are." We have to worry over his problems because if we continued to ignore them, these little things would continue to grow until they were like a giant tidal wave that could turn and come rolling back to engulf and drown everyone and everything we stood for in our own self-centered little individual world. How true are the words "No man is an island unto himself"?

A streetcar went by, and the loud clanging of its bell brought me back to the present and my own troubles. That clanging bell brought a recess, an escape from the inner battle of my mind and soul, from that continual question of why was it like this; and for that, I was glad it had been so noisy.

Yes, regardless of what I said or did, I invariably find myself back, face-to-face with the reality of my difference from other people. I have always found myself up against a solid wall of prejudice and the worst kind at that—racial. If you haven't already guessed it, I am a Negro. I am a full-blooded Negro, but I look beyond a doubt as White as anyone in the world. This I inherited from my mother. My father—God bless him—is a typical Negro in color, but my mother and I are what is known as "Whiteskinned" or "high-yellow" Negroes. We are part of a significant segment of the nation's population who have to suffer the embarrassing rate of never being completely accepted by either "Whites" or "Negroes."

Speaking of White skinned and never being completely accepted by either Whites or Negroes reminds me that as a child, my neighborhood nickname was "White Boy." I hated it, but children can sometimes be unknowingly cruel. It's a funny thing, but I believe a dark-skinned Negro's dislike for a high-yellow Negro is a psychological dislike. I firmly believe they are jealous and don't realize it. I know they look upon light-skinned people with a sort of distrust. These are things no one ever said to me, but you realize they are there just the same beneath the surface.

I remember as a child how the neighbors whispered, the gossips talked, and the kids taunted.

The gossips said we thought we were better than anyone else. The kids joked that my father had been White, and the old-timers said when I grew up, I would pass as White. Yes, those old-timers, the ones that sat on the corner and watched the world go by and analyzed its every turn, they were right after all; or was it they who gave me the idea, the will, to change the destiny of my life?

As a child, I was never really ostracized by the other kids, and yet I never had the feeling of belonging. In a sense, let's say, I was partially accepted. I believe this one thing, more than anything else, psychologically gave me an inferiority complex that in later life became one of my hardest battles to win. I say this from fact because in late years, I was told of this by a psychiatrist.

That's why I was so good in school—an A pupil. Feeling left out or rejected by outside interests, I threw everything into my studies, not so much because I wanted to learn but more as an outlet to express myself. In the classroom, I had a defense. I could prove that I was as good or as big as anyone. It was my chance, more or less, to show off by being the best. But once outside classes, I crawled back into my shell, letting others lead and dominate. I guess my life was this way until my late teens when I finally realized what was happening and decided to break myself of this fear.

I am thankful I had a happy home, for I think had I had disinterested parents, things would have turned out far worse. I don't want anyone reading this to get the idea that I was an unhappy or brooding child. Quite the contrary, I was a very happy child in a good life. These are all strange thoughts of the mind, subconscious worries and anxieties that I didn't fully understand until years later, much later.

Earlier in this book, I stated that my fight, my racial troubles, started when I was born; and I will now clarify that statement. At the time of my birth, we lived on a 125-acre farm owned and operated by my father. This farm was located in a little southern town of Texas where my father, his father, and grandfather before him were born. The family name was well known for twenty miles in any direction. Father was well liked by both White and Negro alike, a great church member, and known throughout the country as a great farmer and baseball player. Bear these things in mind and then explain how neighbors and lifetime friends could suddenly change into gossipy old maids with wagging tongues and embarrassing words as sharp as a two-edged knife. Yet a week after I was born, the rumors and stories had started that will continue to make the rounds as long as I live.

I first heard this from my grandmother—God rest her—who was as White as I am. She told me that my great-grandparents had experienced the same way of life when she was born. Although I knew this story at sixteen, I waited until I was nineteen to ask my father about it. It was as my grandmother had told me or basically the same. My father was more hurt than mad when I told him I knew the story, but he told it to me again with one difference from Grandma's version. He didn't sell the farm and move away because of the talk alone. He sold it for a better way of life for all of us.

Country Negroes at that time were backward and very superstitious, and my father knew it. Both he and Mom finished high school, which in that day was considered the best in education, and neither believed in the supernatural.

Dad knew that the stories or old maids' tales would persist about him and Mom, superstitious Negroes and Whites alike would never let them die. To save all of us future lifetime embarrassment and wanting me to have a good life with the good education, he decided to sell and move to a large city. The larger the city, the more people mind their own business instead of their neighbors. There I received my education and lived sixteen years. Dad took up a new position in which he went to the top and retired eight years ago, and Mom has had a happy life and home. Permit me to change that to say we have all had a good and happy life—thank God.

I was more disgusted than mad, and it was only after reading a Sunday want ad that a way to beat this situation opened before me. The ad was for an inexperienced young White man to learn a new-and-coming trade with good chances for advancement. Upon reading this, I made a decision that was to change my entire life. I was looked upon as a freak in the Negro race and deprived of the free rights of the White as long as I continued to remain Negro. With this thought in mind, I decided then and there to cross over on the other side of the fence to become White. There were a lot of things to be considered, but basically it was as easy as that.

I would like it understood here and now that I never have and never will be ashamed of my race, the Negro. I changed because I wanted a free and independent life with the right to a respectable job and a decent home. I wanted to buy with my dollar the same enjoyment such as good shows, good parks, libraries, and all the other hundred and one things that the White man's dollar was able to buy.

Throughout this book, you may say I painted a one-sided picture, that I show all the faults of one and not the other. The White man's hand is dirty, and the Negro's is not. This is not true. I readily admit that the Negro's hand is just as dirty. They, like everyone else, have their faults and are equally wrong; but I don't think they are to blame. You ask, How can you be at fault and not to blame? To this, there is a simple but understandable answer. Place yourself in these people's place. For generations, they have been born into slavery or its equivalent—poverty, hate, and intolerance—and from childhood, they build a resistance inside against these things. They are always suspicious of the White man and his ways; they are afraid of him because from childhood, they are taught to fear him.

They were born into a sort of servitude without having to serve yet acknowledging their master—the superrace, the White man. The Negroes' actions are the result of a shield placed before them indirectly by the White man.

When I was a child in Texas, it was normal and natural for our parents to teach us to observe segregation. The teaching was rough, even vulgar in some homes. In others, it was quiet and refined. Those of us who lived in the latter homes learned our lessons of segregation along with our lessons of brotherhood and democracy. We learned all of them, but segregation was first above all else—even before the three R's, we knew it.

Negro children always learned their manners—"No, ma'am," "Yes, ma'am," "No, sir," "Yes, sir," thank you, and please. We learned the Bible and were smart in school, but above everything, we learned segregation first. We didn't quite understand it; but "Don't worry, you will as you grow older." We were taught it was law, not the law or brotherhood or the Bible but the White man's law. We knew it wasn't right or that it didn't fit, but we must never question it or think about it.

If only we had been able to do so. We grew up bitter at the White world and mixed up in our own minds.

I think it is obvious that segregation harms the Negro child. To be set apart, the butt of every joke, and made to feel different will injure the mind and emotions of any child.

To be loved at home and accepted by the world are necessary for healthy growth. No child can mature into a healthy grown-up without this love and acceptance.

I was born under this age-old cloak of oppression and hatred, and now I had a chance to discard it. My first thoughts were for my family and what effect it would have on them. I knew Mom would eventually see things my way, but it was Dad I was worried about. I had never really hurt my father, and I didn't want to now. But there was no other way. I knew what this change might cost me, but I was willing to pay the price no matter what.

With all these things in mind, I applied for the job bright and early Monday morning and, without question, was accepted. The company was a new one with a product for automobile paint that guaranteed the paint or finish of the car against fading or oxidizing, making the paint itself 40 percent harder. This product is now off the commercial market because one of our large automotive companies bought the patent rights and is using it today.

I was to be trained in the application of this product because it required a special skill and technique. The advancement mentioned in the ad was if and when I became experienced, I would have the chance of going on the road, with a company salesman, to train men at setting up new shops. The pay was $27 a week to start. And in 1939, that was good money in Oklahoma.

That night, I had every reason in the world to be happy, but I wasn't. I was sad deep down inside because I knew that I must lose some of the things I loved. I wondered then how many more unfortunate members of my race had been forced to do just what I was doing. You have to give up a lot of things that are dear to you, some things that you can't even explain. You give up a certain way of life.

Some of you reading this may ask, "What has the Negro got to give up?" and you would be surprised at the answer. The Negro has a heritage and record he is proud of. One that shows, at this writing, no Negro has ever been convicted of treason against this country that is making joke of this small freedom. He is proud that—in the few short years of his freedom, less than one hundred years—he has advanced and contributed more than any other race in such a short time. They are proud of their scholars such as Booker T. Washington, educator; Dr. Ralph Bunche, American statesman; George Washington Carver, scientist; Malvin G. Johnson and Henry O. Tanner, artists; Richmond Barthé, one of the best modern sculptors; and Marion Anderson of concert fame, etc. One could go on and on, back through the pages of time, and compile an inexhaustible list of famous Negroes. They pity the prejudice that deprives the race the world of more such men and women.

Yes, you give up a lot. Strange people, the Negro or colored people, as some choose to call them. To be born into the Negro race, you automatically inherit a serenity of convictions—a peace of mind that gives them the power to be outwardly gay when their hearts overflow with sadness and the power to look up and continue life's battle in the face of insurmountable odds. Since the days of slavery and the whip, they have been able to find solace, relief, and hope in singing hymns, spirituals, and blues, sung as only the Negro race can sing them. They have been called lazy, shiftless people, and they still continue to rise up to take their place among the great races of the world. Their laziness is a psychological shield in the mind that has helped them through slavery, oppression, and hate—a shield that can be cast aside at will when there is the chance or the opportunity to move ahead, to better themselves or advance their race. They are proud of their race, not ashamed. They are a proud people, but never have they been an arrogant people which in itself means a lot.

I would like to take space here to give a brief compact history of slavery and the Negro race, beginning with the Romans.

The Romans of old were a wise, talented, and intelligent race of people but with two great faults—religious hatred and slavery. We can all remember reading of Christians being thrown to wild beasts in the Colosseum at Rome while pagan Romans enjoyed the spectacle. Persecution of Christians burned fiercely at times during the first and second centuries. We've also read of the slave markets of Rome; slavery was a great weakness of the Roman Empire. It made the people lazy and cruel and unfit and, in the end, contributed to the fall of the empire. These two things, more than anything else, were a blot upon a great civilization.

The northern coast of Africa has seen a series of conquerors including the Romans. In 146 BC, Rome was one of the first great colonial powers to enslave Africa. In AD 415, the Vandals invaded North Africa and overthrew the Romans. The eastern coast of Africa was conquered and colonized by the Arabs about AD 700. Attempts to conquer Ethiopia failed. Arab traders penetrated the interior in search of slaves and ivory. In 1415, the Portuguese, having freed their homeland from the Muslim, established a foothold in Africa itself. Here begins the modern period of European colonization. In 1441, the first African slaves were transported to Portugal, beginning with the European, and later American, entrance into that most tragic of all business. The Portuguese did little settling in the new land but were content to secure gold and slaves.

The settling of tropical America had an appalling effect in Africa. The sugar plantations in the Caribbean demanded much labor, and the Indians were few and not strong enough for this work. Consequently, tropical Africa became the great labor source. In the United States alone, there are over twelve million Negro people whose ancestors were taken from Africa as slaves. Thus, the first modern contact with Africa was not to Africa's advantage.

We have followed the history of the Negro from his early beginning in African slavery, and now we find him at the threshold of our door, the United States of America. In one respect, America can be thankful for the Negroes' presence here because he was one of the reasons, though not the main one, for the start of the Civil War, a war that took a divided nation and united it as one. Some of you may say, "If the Negro hadn't been here, there would not have been a war." This is true, but for the record, let us clarify that statement. First, the Negro did not ask to come here; and second, without the Negro, the South would not have known its productive value nor the country the wealth it gave.

The Civil War was a tragic war fought between the states that cost nearly a million lives and immense property destruction. One of the first definite issues and cause of this great war was the economic problems between the North and the South. Second to this was a united America, which could not be with the existence of slavery. Some of the Northern States wanted laws to forbid the bringing of any more Negroes from Africa. The Southern States would not consent to this. There were disputes over whether slaves should be counted in levying taxes and in deciding the number of representatives in congress a state should have. This was settled by counting five slaves to three Whites in counting population. The Blacks did not vote, so the Southern Whites had more influence than the North in national government. All the colonies held slaves at first, but since slaves were not profitable in the North from a labor point of view, they were set free or sold while many slaves could be employed in the South. Few people anywhere thought slavery wrong though some farsighted people thought it unwise. One of the strongest enemies of slavery was Thomas Jefferson though he owned slaves himself. About this time, the abolitionist movement started, grew stronger, and won friends for the cause of slave freedom everywhere. In the South and the North, John Brown became a martyr to the Negroes' cause.

On October of 1859, he led a raid on Harper's Ferry, Virginia (now West Virginia), and captured the arsenal there. Brown had hoped to arouse and arm the slaves to rebellion, but instead he was captured, convicted of treason by the state, and hanged.

The Constitution at that time guaranteed the individual the right to liberty, but the fugitive slave had to be returned. Such a conflict between ideal and practice could not persist.

Abraham Lincoln became president in 1861, and the nation was plunged into war. One of the greatest acts of his administration was the Emancipation Proclamation, issued January 1, 1863, by which the slaves in all Southern States were declared free. This paved the way for the Thirteenth, Fourteenth, and Fifteenth Amendments to the Constitution (adopted after the war). The Constitution said that slavery was prohibited and the equal protection of the laws and the right to vote were guaranteed to all, but the conflict between ideal and practice did not cease. Negroes were denied the equal protection of the laws and the right to vote.

The National Association for the Advancement of Colored People (NAACP) was founded in 1909. Its humble beginning was devoted to the defense of Negro rights, in reference to slavery practices still in the South. But as time passed, it took a more determined stand against racial discrimination, and finally it began to attack racial segregation itself. I believe that the important work of the NAACP, not only for the Negro but for America, will receive worldwide recognition in the not-too-distant future.

And so, it was the Negro, of all Americans, a people brought to this continent in slavery, that gave America the chance to show the world the principles on which the democracy of America was based. Thus, America can thank God for the Negro; but the Negro can thank God for America, a country which, through its laws and courts, can set free that which it enslaved.

III

I didn't write and tell my family of my new life; I just moved from the Negro Eastside of Oklahoma City to one of the best White sections in the city, North Broadway. The next morning, I reported for work, and that day was the beginning of a new phase of my life, one that I have never regretted.

Strange, I know, but I fitted perfectly into this new society. Within a week I felt as though I had been a part of it always. I enjoyed everything—the work, the living, and even the people. As to my job, it was perfect, especially considering the fact that had they known I was a Negro, I wouldn't have been able to cross the threshold of the door. I was in a completely new world. A door had been opened to me that I never dreamed existed.

I worked hard at my job, and in six months, I was rewarded with a promotion and my second raise. I was now making $38 a week and was to start on my first road trip with the head salesman with all expenses paid.

The first trip was a short one, to Tulsa and a few surrounding towns, all in the state of Oklahoma; but the second and all succeeding trips took us out of the state. We went east to St. Louis and Arkansas, north to Kansas, and west to Denver, Colorado, and California.

Everywhere we went, I observed the people, especially the Negro and their living conditions. I was making a fair wage and traveling in the best style. I saved money, and every week, I sent some home to my family. I had been home once but not mentioned the fact that I was living as a White, especially when I saw how happy and proud the family was at my having such a good job and doing so well on my own. As a matter of fact, the whole neighborhood knew of my good fortune, and I decided there was no reason the family or anyone should know of my change. After all, I was in Oklahoma, and they were in Texas. There is no need of their ever knowing.

I was happy beyond words mainly, I guess, because for the first time, I knew freedom in every sense of the word. To you who take these things that you fortunately inherited at no sacrifice to yourself, I say "You cannot know what hunger is until you have gone hungry." By this, I mean the average American today takes his way of life for granted as though the world owed it to him. I say to you now, "You are a lucky people. Guard well what you have." Men have fought and fought hard and will fight again for the privileges you accept so lightly—complete freedom.

As someone before said, "All good things must come to an end." And so it was with me. The company was opening a permanent home office in Denver, Colorado, and the Oklahoma branch was to be leased to a private individual. In order to retain my present position, I would have to move to Denver with the company. This I was not in favor of because I had no desire to be that far from my home and family. As a matter of fact, I had become a little homesick for my family and the old neighborhood, and this saved me the trouble of making a difficult decision. For weeks, I had tried to decide whether to go home for a short visit or to go for an indefinite stay.

I hated leaving Oklahoma, the life and the company, but when they moved, I left also. I certainly didn't look forward to what I knew was ahead, but I was willing to try again.

Before leaving Oklahoma City and that part of my life, I would like to relate a few personal incidents that happened there because it deals with both the Negro and the White race and because it is a certain part or my life that I will never forget—and I never cease to be amused remembering it.

I find it amazingly funny now remembering how surprised I was at seeing Negro policemen. This was something new, and to me, it seemed as great and important as one of the Seven Wonders of the World.

When I first came to the city as a Negro and before I changed to White, I lived on the Eastside, off Second Street, which is the little Harlem of Oklahoma City. Most second-rate hotels at that time were part-time cathouses and generally run by women or madames, whichever you prefer. The one I chose to live in was no exception though I didn't know it when I moved in, and as in most, they also sold bootleg whiskey.

In all fairness to Oklahoma City, I am neither for nor against a dry state. It's just that I am one of the old school who believes if a man wants to gamble, he will, and no amount of laws will stop him—at least they haven't. This also applies to liquor and women. I will say this though: I hate to see the state and federal government lose all the tax from legal whiskey that could help John Q. Public's pocketbook because you can still see as many drunks and get as much whiskey in Oklahoma City as in any "wet" town equal size. The public should think about this before voting any city or state "dry." Vote a town dry, and the liquor still flows freely though not openly and "nobody" benefits from it.

I wasn't living in the hotel a week before I fully realized what was going on though it bothered me not in the least. I was just young enough to appreciate and enjoy the excitement.

The girls were with their bland, unpretentious honesty and their show of pride toward their work. (Yes, I said *pride* because in my book, I can find no better word to explain it.) I have seen hustling girls the world over, of every description and kind. Artists and authors alike have described them most commonly as has-beens, drunk dope addicts, women that have sunk to the pit of degradation—in short, a sore on the face of mankind and someone to be despised and ostracized. Not so these girls that I knew, both White and Negro. To them, it was a job and a business, and most of them could buy and sell the gentlemen they were sleeping with. I will tell you more about this later, but first I want to speak on morals.

Foremost I would like it understood that I didn't go around with any of the girls and I slept with none, yet I was treated and liked as a friend, more so than their paying customers were.

To further clarify my feeling on this matter before every clergy and civic leader in America yells for my scalp, I am against prostitution of any kind, but—and here is the difference—I have more respect for a woman who says "I'm for sale. I support myself this way. For my favor, you pay me money" than I have for the socialite, the smug rich, and the good, hypocritical neighborhood girl or woman who goes out and sleeps at least once a week with whatever Tom, Dick, or Harry she happens to be with. Yes, sleeps with him and for nothing. These things happen whether we like it or not. One is sinning for a livelihood and the other for hypocritical pleasure. This is also subject to debate; maybe they both receive some sort of pay.

The conditions exist nonetheless and will continue to do so; I just wanted to set the record straight and to explain my reeling in the matter. It's still something that everyone must decide for himself. I don't want to start an argument on the subject; after all, look at the controversy Kinsey started.

To better explain why I say White and Negro girls—and there were both, though not in the same house—there was what is known as a "call girl" system. The call girl system in this case worked differently. In that, the hotel had permanent girls living there, but if a Negro wanted a White woman, one could be called from uptown from a White hotel. Before some of you are up in arms, let me say it worked the other way also. It worked to the percentage that for every Negro requesting and getting a White woman, there were three White men requesting Negro women.

Some White men hide their real feeling with a good laugh, behind the old joke "Get a nigger and change your luck." Whatever the reason, the facts still state that a much larger percentage of White men have Negro women than Negro men have White, and I believe it would be higher except for society and the laws of propriety.

On the other hand, let's analyze one great Southern politician's words in reference to integration; and I quote, "The reason the Negro wants integration and to outlaw segregation is so he can marry our White women."

I don't think the gentleman is right, but who am I to say? Though I do know it was a stupid statement to make. Look at his words; think about them. Is the White woman like a child who has to be protected from her own fellow to begin with? Is she a child?

No. She is a woman who should know her own mind, and she is free to do as she sees fit. It would seem as though the White man is afraid to give the Negro equal rights because he is "afraid" of inter-marriage and that his women would "want" it. I don't believe this. It's sheer ignorance. Better still, it was ignorance that made that state-ment, and I prefer to leave it as such.

Throughout this book I can only state facts and happenings as I saw them. Though you may take issue with some, nevertheless, they are facts; and I have neither added nor detracted.

This may seem to be an odd statement; but living in that hotel, surrounded by prostitutes, I learned more the true meaning of the word *honesty*. I developed a lifelong hatred for hypocrisy of any kind. Be whatever their faults, hypocrisy was not one of them. They were neither proud nor ashamed, but they made no bones about their life.

There were a few that were drunkards though they never lasted long, and some were content to go on just as they were. But the majority wanted something better and were doing this to get it.

One in particular that I remember was Hazel, a White girl and beautiful by any standards. Hazel had come from a broken home and, after innumerable hard knocks from life in Reno Street, became a prostitute at the age of eighteen when most girls are enjoying life and looking forward to marriage. With her, it was strictly business, a means to an end. She had been at it for over four years when I met her and had saved practically every cent she ever made and owned a new car.

The life of a prostitute is short from a health point of view; and after so many years is in the business, she starts to, shall we say, degenerate fast. Hazel knew it and was planning against the day when it would come for her, and I am happy to say she made it. She is still in the state of Oklahoma today, married to a husband who, though he knows her past, loves her; and she truly loves him. They have one child, live in a beautiful neighborhood, and, above all, she is happy. Maybe there is something in what they say about a prostitute making the best wife.

We have continued to be the best of friends, and the last time I was in Oklahoma, I went to see her. I couldn't help but admire and laugh when she said, "Wouldn't some of these rich bitches in this neighborhood boil if they knew my history?" She was still the same Hazel—unashamed, outspoken, and honest.

Fortunately, the hotel was never raided for girls, but it was for liquor even if it was just for show and publicity for politicians. I say this because, though it was raided three times during my stay there, they never found any liquor or arrested anyone.

There was always a tip-off beforehand from someone, and everything was moved out. By the time the raiding party arrived, there was only the ever-present smell of liquor and nothing else. The hotel paid for protection, a shakedown, and they were never caught red-handed, so to speak.

I hated to move from the hotel, and I even missed it for a while. But one thing I never missed was the eternal smell of liquor that goes with a bootleg joint and the Lysol smell that went with the girls.

I never smell either one today, but that it brings back memories—both good and bad.

IV

So it happened that almost two years to the month, I was back where I had started—Texas. Time moves on! Oh, no. Time stands still. We move on.

I would like to explain here that the northern part of Texas is as liberal as or better with the Negro than any of the Southern States east of the Mississippi. The conditions in those states are deplorable, and I freely admit Texas is a little better in the way of living conditions and education. Integration will not find too hard a time there. I pray.

My neighborhood had not changed, and I found it quite easy to adjust myself to the old life. The city itself had changed due mainly to the fact that it was moving to the tempo of war. Everyone everywhere was discussing the war in Europe, and business was fast converting to the implements of war. Jobs were plentiful, and I immediately took one at the new consolidated bomber plant at the lake. They were building huge bombers, and I was put to work in the warehouse as unskilled labor though I mentioned I had majored in woodwork at school. I say this without prejudice, but at that time, woodworkers and carpenters of all kinds were at a premium and greatly in demand. I could see the handwriting on the wall; I was being pulled down in the same old hole I had tried so hard to escape from. But nonetheless, I was willing to fight. After a while, I began to see and get the same treatment as before, and I was still willing to accept it. It wasn't until three incidents had happened in rapid succession that I was ready to admit defeat. I had been back over six months when war was delivered with Japan. I'm sure none of us can forget that fateful December

7. My friends and relations were enlisting every day, and I had waited this long only for the sake of my mother.

Good money was to be had everywhere; consequently, some Negroes were tasting the fruits of good living for the first time. It was only natural that some would invest in a nice home, and therein is where the first story lies. A Negro family had bought a home on the South side. Although it was for sale to the Negro by outside interests, it was considered too close to a White neighborhood by those living there. Nevertheless, it was purchased, and the family moved in. A month passed, and peace reigned. Then one night, a loud explosion was heard by half the city. You guessed it—someone had planted dynamite and blown up the house. Luckily, or by the grace of God, the family was out for the evening. No one was hurt, but the house was a complete wreck. There was the usual amount of publicity, pledges, promises, etc.; but nothing came of it.

If a Negro buys a house in a White neighborhood, the people become panicky and immediately try to sell, often losing in the deal. If they'd wait, they would get their price because of all the Negroes who want to get a house, but they sell and lose because of their own prejudices. It isn't always true that Negroes bring down property values; they often live in run-down houses because that's all they can get. The Negro-congregated housing pattern is directly responsible for an evil overcrowding in which disease and crime flourish. This same pattern is a main factor in continued segregated education despite the Supreme Court's ruling banning such segregation. Even in states which have long forbidden separate schools, segregation in housing breeds Jim Crow schools and many other disadvantages which befall minority groups.

Once the Negroes get into a White section, any number of things could happen. If the section is on the decline, the decline continues; but on the other hand, gross rentals go up because of overcrowding. Sometimes a White street has changed to Colored, and the street stays as neat and attractive as before. In the wealthier neighborhoods, the Colored, if they can afford it, move in many times without creating resentment or changing values. Most property loss is due to prejudice, not depreciation.

From the long-range point of view, the covenants probably aid in depreciation because they encourage prejudices. All Americans have the right to live wherever they please; no one person or group of persons has the right to dictate who their neighbors will be. Nonsegregated housing does work, and prejudice disappears when neighbors know each other as people.

The second episode followed relatively close to the first. A Negro coming from work at the consolidated bomber plant was standing in line, waiting to get on a bus. The White men entered the line and pushed him out with the curt warning that a nigger should get on last, at the end of the line. Even if they were right, with 1,500 employees getting off work at the same time, it was out of the question. A fight ensued, and a near race riot followed. The Negro was found at fault, fined by law, and later fired.

I was thoroughly disgusted with everything by now, and when the third incident struck my own family, that was the end. My mother and father were on their way to a movie, and as they were passing a café, a drunk came out.

Looking first at my mother and then at my father, he asked in a loud surly voice, "What's the nigger doing with that White woman?"

Someone in the crowd answered, "She's a nigger too."

This was the limit. What could my father do? Speak up for his rights? Fight for his wife? No, because he was in the South, in a White man's world. Instead, he must bow his head and humble himself; he must take and accept open insult.

Much progress has been made in securing the right of every citizen to a fair trial and equal treatment by the courts; but unfortunately, as recent events have shown, a sheriff can still shoot a handcuffed Negro prisoner and escape with impunity by claiming "self-defense." A Negro can be tried for "assault" for looking at a White woman one hundred feet away, and a Negro can be put to death for a crime that no White man pays a similar penalty for.

In all sections of the country, a Negro accused of crime against a White person gets harsher penalties than a White person so accused. Rarely in the South is a White person convicted of a major crime against a Negro regardless of the evidence.

I had all I could stand. I had to get away and so decided to enlist. As I was here once again, my hands were tied; or rather, I should say, "my hands were my keeper." Due to my fingerprints, I would have to enlist as a Negro. At any rate, it was a start, and I had to take it. I could travel, see new places, and meet new faces; and if, God willing, I lived through it, I would start over as "White" someplace else—this time for good.

Perhaps you may come to the conclusion that I was a coward in running out on my family and my race, and maybe you are right.

This I don't know and will never know. To my way of thinking, I did the right thing, the only thing. I believe that in so many small ways, I can better help my race by, shall we say, working among my enemies. I believe every deed, no matter how small, helps the cause of racial tolerance and brotherly love. It is the same as a thousand people in a large room of complete darkness, and each one lights a single match. Combined, they create a single light greater than any one person could ever hope to make. My idea was, and still is, to strike many of these small single matches as possible.

Some of you would say "If he had the guts, he could make the world acknowledge him his God-given rights." And again I repeat, "For every Negro who reaches the height of success, there are untold thousands of good qualified men that fall by the wayside." This is why so many before me have done as I did because they were not only interested in their own success but also the success and betterment of our race. Few people know it—and maybe I shouldn't mention it here—but since a well-known magazine has already carried the story, I can see no harm.

In our Capitol at Washington, DC, there is a large percentage of Negro political figures passing as White. In their own way, I hope and pray that they have found the opportunity to strike a few matches—a chance to strike a winning blow at bigotry, racial hatred, and intolerance. Some of you will say this is propaganda as I heard some say about a recent book on anti-Semitism. I can't stop you from saying it, but if you do, I pity you with all my heart. We need more of the printed word on these subjects and more people to read and understand them.

Before going on, I would like to take time and space here to review a few reliable facts that not many Americans know. It stands to reason that because of the conditions under which the Negro is forced to live, he would join the communist party, but few Negroes do believe in the communist doctrines. In spite of it all, they still believe in America; Negroes have no desire to be controlled by a foreign state. The communist party in this country tried hard to get Negro support. They spent more in their efforts than any other party did, but they failed.

Have you ever wondered how many Negroes are in America? There are 16,250,000, and they spend about $16,000,000,000 annually. In 1945, the average income of Negro city dwellers was 66 percent of average White city dwellers' income. The proportion has since declined; but Negro average income, both urban and rural, has increased. The unemployment rates for Negroes are 50 percent higher than for Whites. New factories open, but they want Negroes only for janitors etc. Negroes are generally hired last and fired first. It is true that radio and television are doing a lot for the "talented" Negro, but there are practically no Negro announcers or executives. There are no Negroes employed by the trains or airlines except as porters, waiters, etc. Also it is true that the number of Negroes employed as "white-collar" workers and craftsmen rises, but the percentage is still less than one half of the Whites. In professional occupations, it is less than one quarter.

Man must work if he is to eat. Denying man a decent job because of his race is denying him the basics of his life. Fair employment laws have been passed in fourteen states, but thirty-four states still have refused to do anything about bias in employment.

Is it any wonder that in this great United States of America of ours, there are over 100,000 Negroes "passing," as we call it, as White. It has been conservatively estimated that since the end of the Civil War, more than 10,000 persons of Negro blood a year cross the color line, passing as White. When a Negro successfully "passes," he leaves behind all the restrictions, prejudices, and humiliations he was a victim to as a Negro. Some changed of their own accord; still others were forced to because of innumerable reasons. On this same subject,

41

the percentage of Jews who have changed or passed is abnormally high, especially when you consider that they have been given a better chance at freedom than has been given to the Negro.

Why must these people, these Negroes and Jews, hide their identity? Why are they forced to deny their birth, their origin? These are things that our government and we, the people, must answer and remedy here at home, within our borders, before we can even attempt to lead other nations, the world, out of darkness.

I bring these things out for that great number who ask, "What can I do? I'm only one against a host of many." You can do much. You can strike as many matches, no matter how small, as often as possible; whether once a day or once a month, they all help. Together they can change the tide of battle and lick it, but I ask all of you to remember that the blind fanaticism of one foolish honest man may cause more evil than the united efforts of twenty rogues. Remember a government is only as strong as its people make it. It can accomplish nothing without the aid of its people. If you will help run our government in the American way, then there will never be danger of our government running America in the wrong way.

Some of you will ignore these facts completely because you feel as though they don't concern you because you are one of another race. To that part of society, I say this: "Don't be deluded into this false sense of security. This lying peace of mind." The Negro and the Jew have been discussed here because I knew them; I have played, worked, and lived with them. But this same trouble exists in other races though not quite so bad. Right in Boston, Massachusetts, our cradle of liberty and freedom, there exists a deadly hatred between the Irish and the Italians. The Irish use the joke that there isn't much difference between an Italian and a nigger except that one is a little cleaner than the other. In Texas, the White says about the Mexican, "He's a high-class nigger." These jokes, no doubt, get a good laugh; but what a sadistic sense of humor some people must have to appreciate them.

There is hardly a country in the world whose people are not found here in America, and certainly their loyalty to their adopted country is unsurpassed. Most of them came to seek some kind of freedom, and the majority found it. But not all came to be free. The Negro came to be a slave, and his history in America is one of the most tragic stories of mankind. In 1883, he was emancipated but not made free. He still lived and has continued to live under oppression; but Americans tell the world that the Negro, day by day and year by year, grows freer and that the walls of segregation are crumbling into dust. Is this true that the Negro, at last, is to become an American in every sense of the word? Is he, at last, to enjoy the rights and privileges that Americans enjoy? Will it happen in the not-too-distant future? These are questions I ask myself and you. All I can answer is that the future is full of hope more so than ever before.

When I was in the South, Negroes were forbidden to enter the "White" state universities; now there are more than two thousand enrolled. At this writing though, there are still five states which exclude Negroes. Despite segregation, the Negro in the South has enjoyed one benefit though somewhat belatedly. In 1896, the Supreme Court of the United States ruled that segregation was not unconstitutional provided that the Negro was given equal facilities. This separate but equal doctrine took firm root in the Southern mind, but they rather ignored the equal part of it until the '40s, when several Negro schools were built and White and Negro teachers' salaries equalized in many parts of the South—Texas being one of these.

The United States Supreme Court has declared, in its historic May 17, 1954 decision, that segregated education, impairing the ability of Negro children to learn and to function as responsible citizens, deprives them of their rights under the Fourteenth Amendment and is, accordingly, unconstitutional.

The South is beyond question a different place from what it used to be. The Deep South of the Ku Klux Klan, murder, violence, and the worst discrimination is slowly disappearing. Its theories of White supremacy are gradually being wiped out. World opinion, the constitution, the courts, and the determination of the Negro to become a true American are forcing the Deep South to reject their so-called White Supremacy.

The growing strength of the Negro vote—it has risen from 250,000 in 1940 to 1,250,000 in 1952—could mean the end of the one-party system in the South. The Negro vote will be given to the politician who pledges himself to end discrimination. Recognizing that Negro Americans, voting in free elections, could contribute to winning the rights and privileges guaranteed to them under our constitution, the South, for many years, disfranchised the Negro voter through "White primaries," the poll tax and other subterfuges, and violence. Now American justice has cleared the way for Negro voting in the South with Supreme Court victories outlawing "White primaries" and other tricks. Under constant attack by the NAACP and others, the poll tax is now required in only five states.

The Negro is a minority group to the North and to the nation as a whole; he's only 9 percent of our total population. On the other hand, he is far from a minority group to the South, considering he numbers 25 percent of the Southern population. The 25 percent represents a strong balance of power. This is the real reason the Southern Whites are afraid of the Negro and his right to vote. When he gets that right and integration gives it to him, the crooked Southern politicians and the unfair laws will go under to the voting strength of the Negro.

To get a better look at the North and South Negro population, I did a little research. There are 1,000,000 Negroes in Texas and only 500 in Vermont. In Alabama, there are about 1,000,000 compared to 1,000 in Montana; and in Mississippi, there are about 1,000,000.

Of the 10,500,000 Negroes in the South, about 3,350,000 are boys and girls of school age.

My enlistment in the US Navy was routine, and after the usual red tape, I was on my way to New Orleans, Louisiana, for boot training. Two days later, I arrived at a huge new army camp located under the Huey Long Bridge, a beautiful structure. The coast guard was to use part of the camp until the army completely moved in. My training was like all boot camp training, exercise, drills, Morse code, and a lot of *The Bluejacket's Manual*, the navy's bible. Being a Southern camp, segregation was practiced.

Not knowing when I enlisted, I thought steward mate or mess boy was a respected job for anyone. To my utter dismay, I found I was wrong. This was a "typed" rate. Only Negroes and Filipinos held it although when there became a shortage, near the end of the war, they pressed Whites into this rate.

This I felt, and still do, was quite a blow considering you were branded even by the government and country you were fighting for. In July of 1948, President Truman issued an order in which he declared equality of treatment and opportunity in the armed services, but a lot of good it did me then, considering I was discharged in 1945. On July 21, 1951, the army stated that integration was being practiced in Korea. By the end of 1952, all Negro units were completely abolished in the air force. Today 98 percent of the Negroes in the army are in integrated units. At one time, a Negro was first a Negro and then a soldier. But stories of his unselfishness, heroism, and death became a sore spot on the conscience of America. This so-called inferior man showed such a willingness to die for his country, the country that considered him inferior, that it was just impossible to discriminate against a man who, though you oppress him, still fights for you.

I tried to get my rating changed all through the war without success. How I envied those Negro boys who had enlisted up North as seamen and later went on to boatswain's mate, gunner's mate, etc. Although I went as high as possible with my rate, steward first class, I am still dissatisfied. That rate was the equivalent of a first-class cook, but in the true sense, you are an officer's butler or, better still, a combination of chambermaid and waiter. Yes, I put three ships behind me and a lot of battles serving "soup." If you had to, you would do as I did, "serve faithfully"; but would you want the job? Would you be satisfied? The job itself is all right; it's the idea—the idea that it's such a lowly job that only Negroes are qualified for it.

My time in New Orleans was short, and for that reason, I say it was sweet. Being there twenty-eight days, the first twenty-one restricted, I only made two liberties in New Orleans itself. On those two liberties, it struck me as being a very beautiful and colorful city; and for this reason, I hope to visit it again someday. New Orleans, Louisiana, is the seat of Orleans Parish and the largest city in the state. It is noted for many things, particularly for its fascinating French Quarter, its yearly Mardi Gras, and the Sugar Bowl football

45

games. It is highly important as a port and was first settled in 1718 by the French and was named for the Duke of Orleans. Until 1849, it was the capital of Louisiana.

On my twenty-eighth day, we were told there was a draft of 157 men, both White and Negro. Destination—Boston, Massachusetts. I was part of that draft. It took three days to get to New York where we laid over five hours and then to Boston. We were met at Back Bay Station by half a dozen enlisted men and chief boatswain in charge and, after checking of papers, were marched to the receiving station (the old Brunswick Hotel). All of us were assigned room and bunk for the night and told that the majority would be assigned ships in the morning.

That morning was a fateful one as we later found out. Of the sixty or so assigned ships that day, twelve were destined for death in battle within a month and on their first trip.

Along with three others, I was assigned to a cutter doing convoy duty. Our homeport was to be Boston.

There was a young kid with me from New Orleans that I eventually came to know and like very much—Negro by birth; only five feet, two inches tall or so; and so young his family had to sign their consent for him to enlist. Although he was not quite seventeen, Lewis was still a man in every sense of the word. I say this because after completing our first trip to Iceland, we arrived back in Boston to receive sad news. Most of the sixty men that went aboard ships from boot camp drew convoy, cutters, or troop ships. A large number of these men were from New Orleans, and Lewis knew most of them. As you can imagine, it was quite a blow when we heard that two of the boys killed were, in reality, as close to him as his own relatives. All three had been raised together and had lived all their lives not more than a block apart.

Yes, all this was quite a blow to a kid who had never been more than a mile away from his family and friends. He took it pretty hard, and the next day, I accidentally came upon him crying in the officer's pantry. I couldn't give him much comfort, but feeling for words, I stumbled through something like "This was war, and those that are left must carry on for the future, that God was good, and he had willed for these things to happen in this way. But for the grace of Him, it could have been either one of us. Everything happens for the best, and I told him that I felt death is but a natural consequence, a fate of all on earth. The more I see of it in my family, the less I fear it. I believe it is but a transformation, holding grief and sorrow only for those who remain to mourn the loss of friends or family and bringing peace to the departing one. To me, death has lost its terror. It is only a separation for a while. I grieve over a parting at death as I would for one who is about to leave on a long journey. Time will bring us all together again in the great beyond. I believe God is nature, and nature rules eternity as well as the earth. I believe in universal salvation, and I think that in the life to come, the welfare and happiness of each and every one has been provided for. I say this to try to convince you that death is not so terrible and that your friends have simply gone before you and you will meet them again in time."

This stopped him from crying, and slowly he recovered composure enough to thank me. I was glad to get out of that pantry, but thereafter, we were the best of friends.

When I first came aboard ship, there was the usual whispering among the crew about my difference, my looks, and the never-ending stares of wonder and disbelief. While at sea, I met and talked with practically everyone; and by the time we returned to Boston, I knew and liked the whole crew. I won't say they all liked me because they didn't. There were some who suspected that I would pass myself as White ashore, and they were right. There were others who were just plain rebel White Southerners. Still, some actually liked me, and I made some good friends. There was one machinist mate from the hills of old Kentucky who had no love for a nigger. He had even bragged to a few that his father helped lynch one. Then on the other hand, there was Cliff, a coxswain, and Pee Wee from Upstate New York who accepted me as I was. We were great fiends throughout the entire war and made liberties ashore together whenever possible. Of the six Negroes aboard ship, I was unanimously accepted by them. Basically, though, as a whole, there was always harmony among the complete crew. When we reached port after our first trip, I took liberty with Lewis and another kid from New Orleans. The usual paint-the-town-red attitude of the navy prevailed, and a good time was had by all.

This being my first liberty in Boston, I found everything fascinating; and by the end of our three weeks' stay in port, I had a definite plan toward the future. Out of all the states and cities I had lived in or visited, Boston was foremost on my list. If things went well, I intended to settle down here and live, really live. For the present, I would be a Negro aboard ship and a White man while on liberty. Although this was Boston, even here, there was embarrassment and prejudice to be found.

Whenever I was with Negroes, there were always whispered words and actions, the meaning of which no one could mistake. I remember once being in town with a Negro girl when a White woman brazenly stepped forward in the Park Street subway and flung the remark "You only lower yourself. Why don't you find a girl of your own race?" I was more embarrassed for the girl than myself because I was used to hearing things of this kind.

Needless to say, I began being seen with Negroes less and less. Strangely enough, the Negroes aboard ship never held this against me; maybe it was as Harold, a man of forty from San Antonio, Texas, explained, "I have been born and reared under the White man's oppression. Probably I will die under it, and I fault no man for trying to escape or get out from under it." With this piece of advice, I vowed to break away once and for always.

I spent the better part of my second trip talking and asking questions of fellows who had spent a lot of time in Boston.

The outcome of this was a decision on my part to take my liberties alone with the civilian population and to create new and lasting friendships with as many in and around Boston as possible. This I did and have continued to do ever since.

Upon returning to port, we were told we were going into dry dock and would be in port for over two months. This was heaven-sent news to me because it meant I would be granted leave to go home. I was one of the first to go and was granted twelve days. There were two reasons for me to be happy that I was going home. First, the family had not seen me in my uniform. Second, I was anxious to get their approval on the new life I proposed to live, but I was home three days before I found a chance to mention it.

Dad and I were at the lake, fishing, and it was him who broke the silence. It was unexpected, but I was glad. Point-blank he asked if I had found a part of what I wanted. I was quick to seize the opportunity of explaining bit by bit my future plans, but when I had finished talking and looked at my father, I knew in those short moments he had aged immeasurably—not outwardly but inside, in the mind and the heart, and it plainly showed in his eyes.

For a long moment, he said nothing and just sat gazing at his cork floating there on the smooth lake; and still not looking at me, he said, "I guess your mother and I have been afraid of this moment since the day you were born. Though neither one of us ever spoke out, it was there all the time. Subconsciously, maybe, we said it would never happen, but I think down inside, we both knew it would.

"It's here now, and I don't know what to say—what can I say? A man raises a son knowing full well that someday he will lose him to his own family. He will marry and move away. You expect that and can understand it, but this, this is different. The other way, you lose him, and yet you don't. You know and understand the person, his wife, that you lose him too, but this way, there is no consolation for losing him to the world. Oh, I'm not faulting you. God knows I can't blame you after having lived under the conditions you have. It's just that it hurts and hurts deep, and I'm not ashamed to admit it. I pray your mother doesn't take this too hard. Better let me tell her. We were always a pretty close family.

"I'm not going to lecture you, William. You're too old for that now. I just want you to be happy. That has always been our first concern, and if you can find happiness this way, I'm for it. Never forget though that wherever you go, whatever you do, your home is here, paid for, and you can always come back."

As he finished talking, he sanctioned my desires with the proverb I mentioned before, "Son, our children come from us but not of us. They may have the same color, hair, or eyes that match ours, but they have not our minds. Their happiness comes first before our personal feelings." That is my father's way, and I knew he was giving me his blessing and best wishes for success and happiness in his own way.

As for my mother, as all mothers are, she was generally always in favor of my doings, and this was no exception.

I can remember that day as though it was last week or last month when in reality, it was sixteen years ago. I know now that though I travel the world over or grow as old as Methuselah, I will never forget a moment of that heartbreaking scene. I didn't know or realize then how much that parting in life hurt my father; I do now. "I'm sorry, Dad."

When we are young, there are a lot of things we fail to see. I realize now that this must have been a hard decision to make for both my parents, but they made it thinking only of me and not themselves. Not that I ever disowned my parents. God knows I love them too much to do a thing like that, but think how you would feel if your only son told you that he was going to deny his birth and previous life and become a different person. Not a pleasant thought, is it? Think of just a few things it would mean to you. There would never be any grandchildren for you to spoil and no daughter-in-law to take pride in; and what mother and father, as they grow old, do not want the family gatherings and visits of the children's family? No, it's not a pleasant thought by any means.

This understanding reached between me and my parents made my visit home a complete success, but as time grew short, I found an inner feeling of sorrow at going back. Nevertheless, as Dad said, "This was war"; and after half-hearted goodbyes, I left for Boston.

Now comes a part of my life I can and will never forget mainly because it is the happiest. I arrived back in Boston on a Monday, stood duty Tuesday, and received an early one o'clock liberty Wednesday. Having nothing to do and nowhere in particular to go, I settled for a movie.

Remember these next few incidents because to me, the facts surrounding them are odd in so many ways. I say this and ask you to remember that first, I was luckily granted early liberty; second, my usual way of spending an early liberty with no place to go would be to sleep until supper and then go ashore; and third, it was rare indeed when I went to a movie, especially alone. All the happenings of this day and night were the farthest thing from my mind and intentions. They were not planned. They just happened, and even to this day, I find myself wondering how it all came to pass. It was just the strange work of fate or God—take your choice.

Entering the lobby of one of our larger theaters, I bought popcorn and candy and headed for the balcony. There wasn't much of a crowd, and after looking around, I found a seat in an almost vacant row. In the row directly in front of me, there were three teenage kids; no one over seventeen. The next row in front of them sat a young girl. I was hardly comfortable when I noticed these things along with the fact that the boys were annoying the girl. This I didn't mind too much until they really became fresh and quite loud. The girl had asked them to stop a number of times, and finding myself the only one near enough to help, I asked them to leave her alone. I can't give here the answer I received, but it was enough for me to yank one of them into the aisle and start for the second. By now, a scene had been made, and an usher arrived with a cop in tow. He heard my story, and after a few patrons verified it, the three kids were ushered unceremoniously from the theater. Someone thanked me, and for the first time, I saw the girl's face. She was about eighteen years old with a smile that would soften the hardest heart. Beauty that was further enhanced by her short brown hair with an oval face that looked as clean and beautiful as I imagined an angel would look.

I apologized for the scene I had made and asked if I might join her. She said she was sorry for her part in it and would appreciate it very much if I did.

Yes, that was how I met Mary—in a theater. Maybe to you, it wasn't very romantic; but believe me, it was the sweetest meeting with anyone that I have ever had. Yes, sir, it was wonderful; and for a guy who talks continually, I wasn't able to say anything that really made sense for the next half hour. I finally found words enough to ask her to dinner, and when she accepted, I felt that nothing else in the world mattered. We had dinner in a small café which I knew specialized in Italian foods. I remember ordering an Italian dish that I didn't touch because I couldn't take my eyes off her. If there is such a thing as love at first sight, I had it; and from all outward appearances, she didn't exactly hate me. She was everything I had ever hoped for in a girl—a simplicity of beauty that left you speechless and a warm friendliness that was as much a natural part of her as the blue in her eyes. I knew then if there is a "heaven on earth," being with her was it. These phrases may sound corny, and for that, I cannot apologize because that's how I felt and do to this day.

I saw Mary every day after that, and though we had never discussed it, I knew she felt the same way as I did. About three weeks had passed since I first met her, and all this time, I had been careful to keep our racial difference out of my thoughts. I would have continued to ignore this difference except for a horrible nightmare I had. Maybe it was a guilty conscience; I don't know. But retuning to the ship early one night and being dead tired, I was asleep the second my head hit the pillow. It was a fitful sleep, and I was plagued with dream after dream. In one, I saw myself standing alone in a large room, hearing a voice from someone I couldn't see. The voice kept repeating over and over. "You can't have Mary. You can't have Mary." I kept trying to speak, but I had no voice. When finally words came, I screamed aloud, "I will have her. I will." This woke me up, and I found Lewis and a few of the guys standing over me. I quickly explained that it was only a nightmare, and they went grumbling back to bed. This was the first time I had ever talked in my sleep, and as I lay there cold and clammy with sweat, I wondered how much I had said. There was one thing for certain—I would have to tell Mary everything. She was too sweet and too good for me to go on deceiving. If I loved her, and I knew I did, I must be honest with her no matter what the consequences. I went back to sleep trying to figure a way to tell her, to explain everything.

I awoke the next morning with a morose feeling, a haunting feeling of shame, and one thought—one horrible fear that Mary, the only person I loved more than life itself, would react to the secret as everyone else had and as the world did. By this, I mean she would think herself better than I purely on racial grounds.

Let all who read this know now that there was or never will be anything cheap about our love. Some of you, due to racial pride and human nature, will say she was just "poor, cheap trash." To these few, I can proudly say that there was never a more God fearing, law abiding, and decent, respectable family than the one Mary comes from. It might even have been your daughter I fought for and eventually won as this story will bear out later. Her family is wealthy middle class in the American sense and well respected in the neighborhood.

Remembering these things and knowing with all my heart that Mary loved me, I suddenly realized that a thing like this could never change her. "Why?" you ask. Because knowing Mary and I did, I knew she couldn't be that unfair, that small. A thing like this, a thing born of hate and ignorance, could not change her love for me. I was still the same guy; there was no difference. I was still the same curly-headed guy she had fallen in love with, and with the faith I had in her, I knew that my secret would not change anything between us. Realizing that I was suddenly ashamed that I had not been man enough to tell her before that, I had not been honest with her or myself. Yes, I was truly ashamed, and it really hurt when I faced the fact that until now, I had had no faith in her and that her trust in me had been misused. With the realization of this, my decision was made, and I only waited to see her and make a clean breast of everything to give myself a clear conscience.

I was to meet Mary for dinner, and then we were going to take in a movie. I decided the best time to tell her would be at dinner, in the same little café we went to when we first met. I was to meet her at five o'clock, and I left the ship at two which gave me three hours to do what I wanted. Maybe it was wrong, but I still had a certain feeling of misgiving. I wanted as much in my favor as possible. I stopped at Edward's first and ordered dinner, broiled lobster with all the trimmings. Next, there was a corsage; and last, I bought a necklace, a beautiful single strand of pearls. I figured this way if we parted, it would be something she would always remember; but if she still loved me even after I had told her, then I wanted it to be the happiest memory of our lives.

Deep down in my heart, I knew that if everything went well, this was a forerunner of marriage, and I wanted everything to be perfect.

When we were seated in Edward's, I knew everything was perfect, and I realized I could do no more. It would now be up to Mary, and nothing more I could do or say would remedy that. I opened the box and gave her the corsage, saying it was a lovely flower for a lovely girl. To see her reaction, you would have thought it was the first corsage she had ever received; and for this, I was both proud and happy.

It is here that I ask you to bear with me because I am trying to remember to make you understand every word and every incident.

As soon as Mary found out that I had ordered dinner earlier, she wondered, "'What was the occasion? Why this sort of celebration?" and, as she put it, "Why the solemn face of a funeral" that I wore. I knew that now was the time. I would have to face it all, but try as I might, there was no starting. I felt the small box in my jumper, and opening it somehow gave me the strength to start. Passing the necklace to Mary, I told her it was a remembrance gift, a small token of my love for her. At first, she couldn't believe her eyes. She was happy beyond words, and the smile lighted her face. Though it was beautiful to see, it was like a knife in my heart—I might never see that smile again. As suddenly as the smile had come to her face, it faded with the realization of one word, *remembrance*. Sadly she asked, "Are you going away, Bill?"

With this question, words came as free as the wind; and I said, "Yes, Mary. I'm sailing in about three days, but that isn't the reason for all this."

Before she could answer, I stopped her, explaining that I had something to say and I just wanted her to listen and try to understand completely everything I said.

"To begin with, Mary, I love you. I really and truly do. I love you more than I ever thought it possible to love anyone. Maybe when I tell you what I have in mind, you will hate me. If that happens, God forbid, you can get up and walk out of my life forever. Just remember that I love you now and I always shall, come what may. There are some things that you don't know about me and that maybe you won't like. You say it can't be bad, but please bear with me until I finish. I am not ashamed of my past, what I am, or anything I have ever done. If anything, I am proud although I'm ashamed of not telling you this sooner."

It was here I started feeling for words, the right words. I told her we were different and that regardless of how we felt ourselves, the world would never let us have one another.

"I knew all this when I met you, but I tried to make myself forget, to ignore the fact completely. We were two people born too soon for such happiness in a world ruled by prejudice and intolerance. In some ways, Mary, maybe I'm a coward. I don't know. I only know that because of my intense love for you. I have tried every way to deceive you as to my…my race." My voice was now hardly more than a sorrowful whisper as I continued with "You see, Mary, I am a Negro."

For the first time since I had started talking, I quit toying with my knife; and looking up at Mary, I tasted the bitter fruits of defeat. There were tears in her eyes, and her small mouth was quivering. It was plain enough; here was my answer. There was only one thing to do—leave before we both created a scene. The one thing I feared was happening; she had changed because of my race.

I told her I was sorry, really sorry, and that there was no need of her answering. I would leave. So quick that it startled me, she reached across the table and, grasping my hand, asked me to wait. When at last she spoke, tears were running freely, but words came forth that brought all my dream back to fill my heart with gladness and to make my every wish come true. The joke, and what a joke, was on me. Mary, my darling Mary, had misunderstood me. When I first started talking, she thought I was leaving her and that this was a buildup to tell her it had been only another "sailor's holiday."

In her own words, she said, "Bill, I love you and you alone, not for your race or religion but just for yourself. I am crying, darling, because I'm so happy. I will admit it's somewhat of a shock, but it's not that bad. And when two people love each other as much as we do, they can lick anything. We'll find a way, and we'll come out on top."

Upon hearing this, I was so happy I almost felt like crying myself. There was still a lot to talk about, but there was plenty of time. We had a lifetime ahead of us, and this was something we had to celebrate.

This happened nearly eleven years ago, but I remember every moment of it as though it were yesterday. Needless to say, that was the most enjoyable lobster dinner I've ever eaten.

I returned to my ship that night a very happy man, and the next morning, we sailed.

A grand time in New York City. October 4th, 1943

A lifelong lover of animals, Bill spent time on the family
farm caring for everything from horses to chickens

Being from Texas, Bill was often seen wearing his cowboy
hat and boots, earning him the nickname Tex

Bill and Mary were happily married for over 50 years

Bill and Mary's first apartment after moving
to Brighton, MA in their twenties

Bill as a boy in gradeschool, age 6, in Ennis, Texas

Bill at the kitchen table doing research for his book

Bill in full Legion uniform, age 60

Bill, as a young man in Ennis, texas

Bill's family. Daughters—Carol Ann and Laura.
Son's—Richard and Billy and many granchildren

Bills's mother Mozell, age 78

Mary and Mozell

V

In this chapter, I shall try to tell you of small events and happenings in my life. Some of them concern racial intolerance, hatred, and bigotry that I have witnessed among men. I shall also discuss a bit about integration.

One side of life has been filled with strife, worry, heartache, and toil; but on the other side, there has been compensation in the form of humor. Living as I have, quite often I find myself in the comical position of discussing the Negro race with some of my White acquaintances. I ask all of you reading this to place yourself in my position. Here I am, a Negro passing as White, for which I feel no guilt; and my supposedly good friends sit in my home, drink from my cup, and break my bread all the while telling me that my people, unknown to them, are no good. They are inferior, dirty, ill-mannered; they should be deported to Africa. It's maddening and, at the same time, oh so funny.

This is my laugh at life, my own personal joke. This is also where I get in my licks, my fight for the Negro people. Most of the time, I try to turn the conversation into a sensible, reasonable one, more a debate backed up by facts. I try to show that there is no sound reasoning behind their hate; and more often than I like to see, it ends with their saying, "You're right. I know that inside, but I just don't like them. I don't want to like them."

We are all, in a sense, counterfeiters—experts in the exchange of the true for the false. Man is lost and blinded in the cesspools of his own prejudice. His mind, his body, and his soul has become prisoner with his small racial hate; he is the greatest victim of his own poison, in the depth of a mind so black with poison. No one has to destroy a person who hates, for hate itself will destroy him.

It is true that this book speaks out for the Negro, but feeling as I do in my heart, I have only contempt for racial hatred against any race. Not too long ago, an acquaintance of ours was venting his wrath on the enormous influx of Italians, Greeks, and Jews. His argument was, in his own words, "that America should keep them out all of them. Goddamn foreigners"; yet his grandfather came from Ireland. His hate was anything that they were all coming over here, sticking together, getting rich, and taking good jobs away from good Americana. That is a clouded, ignorant, and hate-filled mind talking. Let's look at the facts; I happen to know why he was mad.

An Italian-owned photography company had just beat him for a large contract to do the layout and photography for one of Boston's large asphalt roof-and-wall companies. It was just that simple, but he wouldn't let himself admit it. Personally, I think the Italian firm was better equipped to do the job, and I am sure the company realized it. Speaking of foreign born, did you know that one in five Americana over sixty-five years old is foreign born compared to one in ten in the total population. Unbelievable, I know, but check it.

Although facts, figures, and statistics are a boring subject and a great percentage of people can't or won't comprehend their full meaning, there are still times when you have to use them.

Thinking along these lines, I did some research on what is an American, who is American, and factually what race or people make up this nationality that we call American. The following population figures are quoted from statistical abstract of the United States in 1955, published in Washington by the US Department of Commerce.

In America today, according to the 1950 census, there are, in round figures, 151,000,000 of all races. There are 135,000,000 members of the White races. This number includes 5,000,000 Jews; 1,500,000 Italians; 2,500,000 Irish; and thousands upon thousands of every other race and country of the world.

In round figures, there are approximately 40,000,000 members of the total White population that are foreigners or direct descendants by one generation of foreigners.

In addition to these figures, there are 16,250,000 native-born Negro Americans. We can't say they are foreigners because there are no African slaves still living in America. You can't say the present generation are true descendants of foreigners because they are placed three, four, and even five generations away from African slaves. Bear in mind when reading this that there is a difference between an African slave and a Negro born in slavery.

Thus far I have spoken of the effect of immigration as a whole on our population. We turn now to a consideration of the origin and composition of our population as it has been affected by immigration.

The results of immigration and foreigners on our population is a complex subject with many sides and one at major interest. Analysis of the total flow of immigration to the United States since 1820 indicates the extent of the contributions of various countries. The proportions of total immigration from 1820 to 1945 coming from different parts of the world are as follows: Of individual countries, Germany has sent us the largest number of immigrants, a total of 6,029,000. Great Britain with 4,269,000 and Ireland with 4,593,000 have been the other chief sources of our immigration from Northern and Western Europe. From Southern and Eastern Europe, Italy with 4,720,000; Austria-Hungary with 3,144,000; and Russia with 3,344,000 have also been significant contributors. In the Americas, Canada holds the most conspicuous place, having sent us 3,059,000 immigrants during this period.

Of the grand total of 38,461,395 immigrants for the period of 125 years from 1820 to 1945, there were 32,678,000 who came from Europe; 922,000 from Asia; and 4,511,000 from the Americas. Of this last figure, about three-fourths came from Canada and about 900,000 from Mexico. The figures for Asiatic immigration indicate that 383,541 came from China and 277,949 from Japan. These figures may be compared with the 1940 population—77,504 Chinese and 126,947 Japanese, indicating the smallness of the residue of Orientals now in the United States.

Native-born persons of foreign stock are increasing in proportion to the foreign born. The census of 1940 shows that an increasing number of our racial minorities are of American birth. It is interesting to note that 75 percent of the total number of German stocks were born here, and the percentage of Irish stock is even greater. Six out of every ten persons with Italian background were born here. The same is true for half the French Canadians in our country. Almost two-thirds of those of Jewish blood are American born.

These figures mean everything to some people, and to others they mean nothing. I have only touched on the population of America and its races of people lightly. I have not even scratched the surface, and yet is it so important when you look at racial hatred with an unbiased mind? Is it right for one foreigner or minority group to trod on and curse another when you consider the simple fact that we were all foreigners to America in the beginning? Only the American Indian is a native-born child, and our forefathers realized that when they gave us the Bill of Rights and wrote our Constitution. These things were all considered, and they made it possible for us all to be first and foremost Americans. Regardless of our racial origins, we would first be Americans in the eyes of the world.

That is as it should be. I only wish that more of us could realize and understand it better. These are the races of people that make up the nationality of America; and yet we curse and hate each other while America, the nation, tries to lead the world out of darkness while she preaches freedom and democracy for all. Does it make sense!

The great claim of the United States and its people is democracy. The White man's argument against integration and equal rights is that nowhere else in the world do dark-skinned people, and especially the Negro, do as well or have as high a standard of living as here in America. The obvious oversight in such comparison is the fact that all White people of our United States also live on a higher standard than any other White people in the world; yet they have the development, the progress, and the wealth with no restrictions. As I said before, no country or individual can be great or just that lifts up one part of its people with one hand while it pushes another part down with its other hand because of their racial or religious differences.

Earlier in this book, I said that my father was a sort of poor man's philosopher; and throughout my life, his teachings and proverbs have influenced my actions greatly. As an example, I remember a story he loved to tell that, though it has no bearing on this book, will help you better understand my youth with him.

The story concerned an old fellow working in the roundhouse for the railroad. Every day he would come in, take his hammer, and start tapping the large train wheels. With one type of sound, he placed the wheel on one side of the building; and with another type of sound, he placed in on the other side.

One day, a stranger came through the yards; and seeing the old man separate the wheels by sound, he asked him what he was doing and why.

To this, the old man replied, "I don't know. You see, I came to work about ten years ago, and the foreman told me that when the wheels rang with a deep bong, they were to be placed on this side, and when they rang with a hollow bing, I should place them on the other side."

Though the old fellow had been doing his job and doing it well for ten years, in a sense, he still didn't know what he was doing or why. The reasons were simple. If the wheels resounded with a deep bong, they were good and should be placed on one side. If they gave a dull bing, it meant they were cracked and should be placed on the other side for repair.

My father would then say, "Now the old man didn't have to know how to build a train, how to run one, or even what made a train move, but he should have known what he was doing and why in order to do a better job."

I try always to remember this little story.

Another proverb that he always quoted was the one by George Bernard Shaw that goes "Choose your friends wisely and carefully because you will find it is easy to have a world of acquaintances but few true friends."

This is the one I went to talk on because it concerns me and racial intolerance.

Throughout my life, I have met and accepted everyone at face value knowing eventually they would prove to be true friends or fair-weather buddies. Following this course of thought, I have had more than my share of social climbers, name-droppers, fair-weather friends, etc. I am sure everyone reading this has had his brush with this type of person. To explain better what I mean, let me tell you one such person.

About eight years ago, my wife and I met a lady who, in time, we both liked very much. She was married with a six-year-old boy whose father was overseas with the US Army. We became great friends, and I eventually found myself eagerly awaiting her husband's return. I had heard so much about him I felt I knew him already.

The day of his arrival came, and I found that he was all his wife had led me to believe. He was a well-versed, intelligent man of high integrity and with a good sense of humor. I freely admit that for a while we all had fun together and got along famously. It wasn't until he was back about six months that I began to notice little things, things that eventually I mentioned to Mary.

First and foremost, though he had been raised in Boston in a Jewish neighborhood, it was a fact that no matter what the conversation in his home was, he would always get the Jewish argument going and run them down in every way possible. It wasn't an argument in the true sense because I generally just sat and listened. It was getting to the point that I hated to visit them, knowing his true feelings and visualizing what the complete evening held. This feeling continued to grow in me until I was filled with a lack of respect for him, but still we continued seeing them. I had known him personally for over a year when he placed the straw, so to speak, that broke the camel's back.

Before going into that, I would like to explain something that will help you better understand the next incident. I am sure that most of us, upon meeting a person for the first time, try from good manners to find a mutual ground upon which to carry on the conversation—about his job, his business, or any number of things directly connected with him. In my case, it has always been, to anyone who meets me for the first time, to say "Texas." There have been the usual jokes, the educational topics, such as size, weather, points of interest, or someone they remember from Texas during the war. All of these I enjoy, but now and then, I am bored with the few that class Texas as the South and use the Negro as mutual conversation ground. Regardless of my feelings, I would like to state that there are thousands of Texans who deplore racial hatred talk against the Negro.

On this particular visit to our friends' home, as usual, everything went well for about an hour; and then the conversation turned to the hatred for the Jew. I was half listening to his fanatical analysis of the Jews but took greater interest when he started on the Negro. I had heard most of his arguments before either from him or prejudiced people like him, but this time, he was saying something that interested me very much.

It seems that in his youth, while traveling around the country, he had spent two years in Georgia and Florida. I don't know if he said it to try to impress me, if he was lying, or what; but there he was, standing before me, admitting that he once belonged to the Ku Klux Klan and, because of hatred for the Negro, had once helped burn a Negro's home. Here before me was a mixed-up, hypocritical man who had no true God or love. He was born and raised with the Jew.

He had married a Catholic girl which, at that time, the Ku Klux Klan was against. He was a Maine Protestant, and yet he took his hate for everything and hid behind a robe and burning cross to persecute a Negro family who had never done anything to him.

I knew in that moment that this man would never be a friend mine. I could never trust him after that. We spent the rest of the evening together, but when Mary and I left, we both agreed to break off that friendship as nice and painlessly as possible. We see them now, maybe once a year, treat them cordially and all that but nothing more.

Some of you reading this will probably say that I have a wrong or mixed-up view of everything and that I am a person who says, "I'm right. If you don't agree with me, you're wrong."

I don't want to create that impression. I couldn't write the things I have without believing in your right of freedom of thought. On the other hand, what I have tried to do is to give you facts and understanding—not my facts but facts of the world, facts on conditions, and facts for the future.

I believe in integration. I must believe in it to have faith in this country's future. I believe there can be no middle of the road, no straddling the fence. You are either for or against not my thoughts and ideals but the principles that have made this country the great nation it is. I say that anyone not wanting integration is wrong. If that's what some of you want me to say, I will.

What we are facing today with integration is simply the tearing down of an old idea—nothing more. It is an idea in the mind. Mainly, this idea, clung to by certain White groups, is that no people who are White are superior to other people and have the right to dominate them. Hitler preached these same doctrines and ravished half of Europe. The world was incensed at the idea. All-out war was declared, and we won it because we were fighting for the God-given rights of mankind—freedom and equality. Are we to believe that Hitler can preach that the German people are the superior race and be wrong yet White Americans preach the same thing and be right?

No, if it is wrong for one, it is wrong for the other. If you agree with this, there is but one answer—integration. It will affect America's external way of life very little. There will be no great loss of lives, no property loss, and no world-shaking financial changes. There will be only the breaking of an emotional deadlock of the mind, like losing an old superstition.

We in America know that the threat of integration is a mythical ghost, nothing more. We know that nothing bad happens when White and Negro go to colleges and universities together. Nothing horrible takes place when they compete in sports; nothing dreadful occurs when they worship in the same church.

Still, there are millions who do not yet understand and believe. They are afraid to give up their old ways. It is a mental block of the mind, nothing more.

Despite this great conquest of nature, man still lives in profound ignorance on fundamental questions of life. We know more about the relations of atoms and animals than the relation among human races or human beings.

The problem of integrating the races, particularly the Negro and the White, is the number one social problem in America today. Brotherhood is something not just to believe in; it is something to live every day.

As I have said before, I was well-liked aboard ship although everyone knew I was passing as White. Everyone except, as I found out on this trip, my executive officer. The following facts I tell you are not from malice of thought nor with hatred in my heart; it is simply the truth. I had always cooked for the officers although I was only a steward's mate first class. My original intention was to try for a petty officer's rating. But they were giving ship's cook ratings to Negroes now, and I had stayed in the officers' galley solely for the chance of going to cook and baker school.

The time to work for your rating was at sea, and I had made up my mind that this trip, I would get it. After being at sea about a week, I approached Mr. Jenkins, my executive officer, about changing my rate.

His first question was "Why, boy?"

To this, I answered, "I want to better myself both in pay and rate, and I know I can pass the test for ship's cook third class."

For the benefit of the reader, I would like to describe Mr. Jenkins as a pupil of the old school of Southerners, born and raised in Mississippi complete with arrogance, prejudice, and expecting all Negroes to act with a certain amount of "Uncle Tom." He was a short shrimp of a man, of stocky build, and with a head that was extra large, so much so in fact that it looked out of place. He was married and had been in the service about twenty-five years. For fourteen months, I watched and heard him call every enlisted man "boy" regardless of whether he was eighteen or forty-five years of age. He addressed everyone as "boy," be he White or Black.

After hearing my answer to his question, "Why, boy?" he just sat there smoking his pipe as though weighing the matter's pro and con. When at last he did answer, it was in quite a different vein; as a matter of fact, it was something I never expected.

Looking straight at me, he said, "Boy, I'm going to give it to you in a blunt way as I should have done sooner. I've been hearing things that I don't like, the way you make your liberties, the people you associate with while ashore."

I was quick to ask what he meant. I had never been in trouble either ashore or onboard ship.

He calmly relit his pipe and continued with the most unorth-odox, disgusting statement I have ever heard any man of any race make.

In a voice that held suppressed anger and hatred, he said, "Pointer, you're a nigger. We both know it, and I don't like the way you're passing yourself uptown as White. We're both from the South, and you know as well as I do that if you ever pulled a stunt like that back in the South, something bad would stop you. You know what I mean. I've heard little stories about you, here and there, and I don't like any of them. And that's another reason why as long as you are on this ship, you'll keep that rating. It brands you as a nigger, and it will keep you in your place. Don't try me, boy."

For the first time in my life, I wanted to choke someone, to throttle that voice, and to twist his head and break every bone in his neck. For a moment, I just stood there clenching my fists so tightly that I could feel the fingernails cutting the palm of my hands. When at last I found words, they came through clenched teeth, sounding more like the hiss of a snake than my own voice.

Common sense tempered my words as I replied in a low voice, "I'm sorry you feel that way, Mr. Jenkins. I came here to ask about my rate, not to discuss my personal life. As far as I'm concerned, I haven't broken any military rules, and until I do, I don't think my personal life is of any concern to you or anyone else aboard this ship."

I could have been court-martialed for this bit of insubordina-tion; but instead, Jenkins pointed to the door and ordered me out with a parting reminder, "You'll never get that rating changed, and you won't get transferred off this ship, at least not while I'm executive officer aboard. And that's final."

I returned to duty with a deadly hatred for everyone and everything.

In a way, it was funny. Here I was fighting for freedom sup-posedly for all mankind, and I was little more than a slave myself. Strange people, the colored people who, through such scorn and rejection, have clung so fiercely to the ideal of America. I brooded over this the rest of the trip, not saying anything to anyone about it. But I knew I had to get off that ship, or else I would get into serious trouble with Jenkins. There is no other word for it; that time, I would have been glad even to kill Jenkins.

This frame of mind still possessed me when we returned to Boston, and on my first liberty, I went straight to the district office, to Mr. Nelson in charge of military morale. I told him the complete story, leaving out and adding nothing, and when I had finished, he was truthfully shocked. He didn't believe that a man in Jenkins's position could carry a prejudiced grudge so far as to openly express himself as he had. Nelson wanted no scandal and no open fight with Jenkins, and he was quick to tell me so. But he did promise that I would be transferred and soon. I didn't like the idea of his covering for Jenkins though I didn't blame him, but what could I do? I was getting transferred, and that was the main thing. Two weeks later, I was transferred to a shore station; and to this day, I have never seen Jenkins again.

Yes, I guess some of you reading this will be skeptical; but nevertheless, it's all true, cold facts with no false show of feeling or emotion. This act or racial prejudice in the armed services was only one of many that I personally know of that happened to many boys of many races. We don't need to check war records and service men. You can see it every day in civilian life. How many times have we seen good men held back, men with real know-how, because of their race? Believe me, Mr. and Mrs. America, we hurt ourselves as well as them. True, the Negro race has come a long way, but it still has a long way to go.

Mary, never having been exposed to very much racial trouble, was shocked upon hearing of Jenkins's prejudiced attitude. She couldn't believe that a man of his type existed, especially here in New England, in Boston.

In a way, I was glad it happened and told her so. I explained to her that this was an example of what lay ahead—a small test of our love because there would be bigger problems of the same kind. I never liked to talk like that because once I was started, I could torture and cut myself to pieces with truths and facts I didn't like. Mary must have seen this because she always stopped me, and this time was no exception.

Placing her hand on my lips, she said, "Bill, I realize the problems we both have before us, and loving you the way I do, the way we love each other, I know we can lick it. Jenkins is something left from the past, something that we won't see in the future ahead. His kind is dying, Bill, where our kind is being born every day. In our school, churches, homes, and the government, and a lot of other places are new people with new ideas and principles and a full understanding of the brotherhood of mankind."

Yes, Mary always stopped me, and why shouldn't she? What she said made sense; and although you know it was a long way in the future, you knew there would come a day when Jew, White, Negro, Italian, Protestant, Catholic, and all the others would stand side by side, equal, and stand side by side with no hate or malice in their hearts for one another, no prejudice—all equal and free in every sense of the word. Yes, when Mary spoke like that, I knew why I loved her. I loved her more because she was good and clean, something that the world of today is forgetting to respect in a person.

My next personal brush with racial intolerance involved Mary's family, my future in-laws. At this writing, I couldn't ask for a more devoted mother- and father-in-law than I have. They are perfect; I am treated as well as their own son. Between us, there is real love for one another; and for this, I am thankful. It wasn't always like this though; at one time, there was deadly hate between us. I seem to be getting ahead of myself here, so I will go back and fill in some of the facts.

The original trouble started quite by accident. After being transferred from under Mr. Jenkins, I received shore duty for about six months. During this time, I was with Mary almost every possible chance I had; and quite often, I was invited to her home for Sunday dinner. It was on one of these Sunday visits that, quite innocently after dinner, I suddenly found myself in the middle of a debate with "Pop" concerning the Jews. It's a funny thing, but to this day, I don't remember how the argument started. But at any rate, as political arguments tend to do, it was soon out of hand. He was strongly cursing the Jews and giving me all the old-age arguments I had heard a million times. I had been discussing the Jew and expressing my views in a sane, sensible way, and it wasn't until Pop called me a "damn Jew lover" that I realized the argument was out of hand. Mary and Mom must have realized this also because about this time, they came from the kitchen to intervene.

They stopped us, but not before I said, "Jew lover or not, that's the way I feel, regardless. As a matter of fact, I know some Jews that I've got more respect for than I have for you."

My father-in-law, being what you call a thick-headed Irishman, took this last bit of argument as a fresh remark from a fresh punk kid and, after telling me so, stomped out of the room madder than ever.

Mary and Mom were upset because they knew Pop didn't forget or forgive easily. As to my feelings, I didn't particularly care, and I told them so. I had lowered myself to the point of a stupid argument on the subject, but other than that, I felt no remorse. Knowing Pop, I knew my welcome at the house was on shaky ground, but I figured that in time, everything would be forgotten.

For about the next four months, I met Mary in town or some other place. When at the end of this time I found Pop's resentfulness at me unchanged, I resolved to make the best of it and to let a sleeping dog lie. Although he knew Mary and I were still seeing each other, he had no knowledge of my true race. It was a good three months before he found out about that.

The Jewish argument had taken place the latter part of January. In June, after having been ashore for almost six months, I was assigned to another ship on convoy duty to Liverpool, England. I liked everything about my new ship. There were even some of my old buddies aboard, and that made it perfect. I guess I would have finished out the war aboard her if not for an accident.

We were two days out of Liverpool when general quarters for airplane was sounded. As I hit the main deck going to battle station, there was a loud explosion, a direct bomb hit. The next thing I remember was my being over the side, in the ocean, with someone on board yelling, "Grab the life preserver!" That was all I remembered although later they told me I unconsciously grabbed the life preserver and hung on until I was hauled back aboard. I only remember waking up below in sick bay and asking what happened. Dr. Cotten told me we had been hit aft by land-based planes that had made a bombing run on the convoy. As for myself, other than being soaked to the skin and shock, Doc thought I was all right. Damage to the ship was slight, and everyone felt sure we would make port okay.

It was a week later, and we had made port before we realized that I didn't escape injury in my dunking. I suddenly began to have severe pains in my abdomen. It wasn't until X-rays were taken that Doc told me my stomach had been injured through water concussion. It seems that while I was in the water, two waves had decided to come together with me in between. The result was that in some way, it damaged my intestines, especially the digestive tract. After the usual red tape and doctor's consultations, it was decided that I would be flown back to the states for medical treatment. I was lucky because two days later found me aboard an air transport command plane headed back for the States and Mary.

We entered the States at Presque Isle, Maine, where I boarded a train for Boston. Although my orders read to report to Chelsea Naval Hospital immediately upon arrival in Boston, the temptation to see Mary was too great; and four thirty found me waiting for her after work.

This trip at sea had shown me all I needed to know as far as we were concerned. We had been apart only a couple of months, but it had seemed an eternity to me. Being with her constantly for six months and then apart for only a little while had shown me how much I needed her, how much I loved her.

Yes, I loved Mary; and believe me, it wasn't hard to do. A girl with skin like cream and soft like velvet, and hair golden brown like wheat in the fields, blue eyes with flecks of green, a sweet mouth, and beautiful hands; and when she walked by, you had to stop and turn just to see the graceful movement.

My thoughts were suddenly interrupted with the realization that girls were streaming past me coming from work. Then I saw Mary, or rather, we both saw each other. The next moment, she was in my arms. I held her close, and in that moment, nothing else mattered. We were oblivious to the giggles and wise cracks of the girls passing by. It was Mary who spoke first and brought me back to the reality that we were standing in the middle of the sidewalk. We both laughed, and taking her by the arm, I flagged a taxi. My time was running out because I was long overdue at the hospital, but I was willing to chance another hour. Once in the cab, I directed him to Edward's, our restaurant, and then locked Mary in my arms for that long-awaited kiss. By the time we reached Edward's, I had explained roughly the past happenings and why I was in Boston. Yes, I took an extra hour; and even if they had court-martialed me, I still would have considered the price cheap. At any rate, there was no trouble over my being late, and seven thirty that night saw me beginning a rugged stay in Chelsea Naval Hospital.

VI

Before going further, I would like to give credit where credit is due—to the men of my ship. As a crew working together, they were perfect. These are the facts pertaining to my rescue that I didn't know of until later. As I was thrown over the side, a Negro seaman gave the alarm "man overboard"; and in all the excitement, an Irishman had the forethought to throw a life preserver. After making a wide circle, my captain, who was a German, picked me up, which in itself was quite a risk under the circumstances. The lieutenant directing the rescue was a Jew. Strange isn't the word for it, but do you fault me for not wanting any part of racial hatred and intolerance? This incident, my rescue, proves what men of different races can do when they work side by side. It proves that it is possible to achieve a brotherhood of man.

I would also like to take this opportunity, with the permission of *Collier's Magazine*, to reprint an article to which they devoted their entire editorial page some time ago in reference to this same subject.

A Challenge to Bigotry

Seven days in February is Brotherhood Week. It has been so designated by the National Conference of Christians and Jews. Today Collier's devotes its editorial page to the calm words of three men—a Protestant, a Catholic, and a Jew. They speak as brothers, sons of God. Read, Reflect. Then with them, light the lamp that will dispel the darkness or bigotry in a bewildered world. All of us are brothers—sons of God.

Harry Emerson Fosdick
Minister Emeritus, The Riverside Church, New York

"Brotherhood," says the National Conference of Christians and Jews, "is giving to others the rights and respect that we want for ourselves." That is the indispensable quality of all people who are fit to live with and being fit to live with is the desperate need of the modern world. It has always been men's crucial need in families, neighborhoods, tribes and nations but within the last few generations, with distance conquered and intercommunication expanded all mankind has been poured into one receptacle until what happens anywhere happens everywhere, and it can never be securely well with any unless it is well with all. We humans have got to live together that is the big MUST for mankind from now on.

As Prime Minister Attlee once said, "We cannot make a heaven in our own country and leave a hell outside." Inescapable propinquity and interdependence are here, personally, racially, internationally, whether we like them or not and it is now a question of brotherhood or else!

It is fitting that the public recognition or this fact in Brotherhood Week should be sponsored by the National Conference which represents Roman Catholic, Protestants and Jews. For while brotherhood can be politically expressed, it cannot be politically created. It is a moral quality, springing from good will and from profound convictions about the dignity of human beings as children of God.

Unless we have such deeply grounded personal respect for men and women, across all racial, religious and national lines, we shall not get the kind of brotherhood that can save the world.

The National Conference of Christians and Jews is trying to get this idea of brotherhood down out of the stratosphere and make it walk the common earth. The brotherhood of man is usually treated as a beautiful ideal far ahead of us. Upon the contrary, it is the hard-headed facts of our compulsory interdependence as members of one human family that have gone far ahead of us.

As former Secretary Marshall put it, "There must be one world for all of us, or there will be no world for any of us."

Brotherhood Week should be taken with special seriousness here in the United States. We represent democracy before mankind. Racial prejudice has no place in it. Every slur voiced by a Gentile against Jews, or by Jew against Gentiles, is sin against it. Economic class-consciousness is the denial of it. To respect others dignity, needs and rights as we want our own respected is the essential Spirit of democracy, and the surest road to the ultimate defeat of communism is to make such democracy work here.

Solomon Goldman
Rabbi, Anshe Emet Synagogue, Chicago, Illinois

The National conference of Christians and Jews may be said to hold the following rarely remembered truths to be self-evident:

1. The main cause of hostile manifestations against minority groups is the resentment

of the unlike. Politics, religion, economics and ethnic traits, to be sure, play their part but they do so only as secondary factors. A minority is hated primarily because it is suspected and feared.

2. Men upheaved by ambition or greed exploit this primitive instinct and conceal their designs in propaganda against or persecution or minorities, even as Hitler veiled his plans against Western civilization in anti-Semitism.

3. The emergency or sudden passion against a minority is more often than not the first rumblings of deep convulsions. Thus, the Jews have ever been the seismograph, receiving and recording the first impact of the shock.

4. Differences among human beings are unavoidable and are probably here to stay. Consequently, every attempt to develop a society of universal fellowship must be based on the recognition that culture and religious divergences are as real as racial dissimilarities. We cannot by coercion bludgeon the world into a uniformity of belief, worship or speech.

5. Men prize freedom above life. By freedom they understand the right to differ, to be in fashion with themselves. To deny them such freedom is to stir up antagonism and engender strife.

6. Though recognizing the inherent fact of human diversity, Judaism and Christianity have both taught: (1) that the highest revelation is that God is in every man; (2) that all men are the children of One Father and

descendant of a common ancestors; and (3) that they are all implicated in a common destiny.

If what has been said thus far represents the thinking of the conference, then its purpose in bringing Christians and Jews together is obvious. It is to increase and multiply that rarest of all species, an unprejudiced human being.

The quest is not an easy one. But the conference is determined not to forget the horror of Europe, the unspeakable martyrdom of 6,000,000 Jews, the heartache and shame of the 20th century's reversion to primitivism.

Can the conference succeed? Postwar pessimism is certainly understandable. But despair is a bitter medicine that brings no healing. The answer to the question is that the conference must succeed. Perhaps if science were to probe into the original tendencies of human nature with the great resolution with which it concentrates on splitting the atom, the day of universal peace and brotherhood might be very near.

John L. Mc MaMon
President, Our Lady of the Lake College, San Antonio, Texas

The times we live in are amongst the most unbrotherly in all history. Our century, not yet through half its course, has rightfully been called the bloodiest of all. By comparison, the wars of an Alexander or a Caesar were but minor battles when measured by the ferocity of our last World War. But the killing of soldiers and noncombatants in unprecedented numbers by the most efficient weapons ever devised is not the only proof of man's unbrotherliness in our times. The sadism of the concentration camp, the forced expulsion of the millions of people from their homes without their adoption by other countries in a new manifestation of racism, the retention of millions of prisoners of war and slave laborers, the unrelieved hunger or three fourths of the people of the earth, the new wars of the East and Near East all bear testimony that the culture of man is sick and that man in his relations with his fellow man has acted and is acting brutishly.

It is in such a world that the National Conference of Christians and Jews seeks to accomplish its noble end the recognition by all men that they are brothers under God and that they must in their relations with one another act, in whatever capacity and on whatever level, as brothers.

Here in our beloved land the National Conference of Christians and Jews, in only 20 years, has done pioneering and successful work in diminishing group tensions and in promoting mutual respect end understanding.

It is not too much to say that because of this work the intensity of such alien movements (alien in both origin and to the spirit of our institutions) as anti-Semitism and anti-Catholicism has been diminished and that the rise of such an organized national hate movement as the old Ku Klux Klan has been made more difficult if not impossible. The conference's work is in the pioneering stage, but through such agencies as its Educational commission, which seeks to know the causes and cure of group tensions and prejudices, and through its projects in the schools, college and neighborhood it is making a daily contribution to better American living.

The National Conference of Christians and Jews has expanded its activities to include many European countries, when it seeks to remove the age-old suspicions and enmities that have characterized too much or European life. It has now banded all its national organizations into an International Council of Christians and Jews because its profoundest conviction is that brotherhood is universal and knows no earthly limits. It believes too, that if a new age is to arise, men of good will of all races and nations must give it their impress.

This is truly an inspiring article, but let us look now at a few statistics.

The past few years have witnessed a great increase in church membership which now stands at 53 percent of our population, the highest in our history. Over seventy-seven million of our people are voluntarily identified with some form of organized religion. Still, for many, church memberships is in name only; the record is so far below the seventy-seven-million mark as to be ridiculous and pitied.

The true picture of the Christian church in America, in regard to race and color, is rather difficult to give.

I have heard vicious anti-Semitic prejudice expressed in men's Bible classes and on the church steps. I have heard sermons based upon "Love thy neighbor" it preached from the pulpit weakly, very weakly, extended into the field of racial discrimination. Whites, Negroes, and Jews of all religions get together for the good of mankind all too little. You cannot further the brotherhood of man by encouraging class or racial hatred.

Some of you will say that I am prejudiced on this subject because I am a Negro myself. To this, I say, "As God in heaven is my judge, I truthfully feel no malice toward the White man or the Jew." I only know that we need to practice joint membership among churches more and to receive members without reference to racial affiliation. I call attention to the goal adopted by the Federal Council of Churches, "A nonsegregated church in a nonsegregated society."

In many cities across the country, the Catholic Church has done much to further integration. Many Catholic schools have long since abolished segregation. Of all the churches in America, the Catholic has shown the most willingness to obey the will of God. Of course, it is true that under the laws of the Catholic Church, it is impossible to leave one Catholic Church and set up another. Although there are separate Negro parishes, there cannot be a Negro Catholic Church.

The Quakers also have a noble record in regard to race relations. Their meetings, schools, and colleges are open to all; but there are still a few exceptions.

Most Negro Christians belong to Baptist, Methodist, or other Protestant denominations; and for the most part, they worship in their own churches. The number of Negro and White Protestants who worship together is very small. It is true that the segregated housing situation in America somewhat hinders the possibility of mixed congregations, but it is also true that the segregated churches do nothing to further the abolishment of segregated housing.

American Christians, both White and Negro, are inclined to ignore the scandal of the racially divided church. The situation is further complicated by the fact that the Negro, who has fought so hard to enter the White schools, the theaters, and restaurants, has no desire to enter the White church. He has made his own church where he can sit where he pleases and listen to a preacher of his own race. Furthermore, he has developed a religion of his own, one of deep faith and love of God. The White world needs to know more of this faith of the Negro, for it is sincere in its simplicity. Perhaps as Christians gradually quit thinking in terms of race, they will go more and more to their neighborhood churches regardless of what "color" it is.

VII

I class my stay at Chelsea Naval Hospital as rugged for two reasons. First because it proved rather embarrassing, and second because it was the forerunner to serious trouble.

My first three weeks were pleasant. I received the best of medical treatment. The rest and sleep were sublime, and Mary visited me twice a week. It wasn't until the beginning of the fourth week that the storm broke.

So far, I had not been granted liberty to go ashore due to the condition and the medical treatment I was receiving. It was the custom that upon being granted liberty, your ward doctor posted your name and rate on the ward bulletin. I was granted liberty. My rate went on the board, and the cat was out of the bag. There was no practice of racial segregation at the hospital, and everyone naturally had taken me for White. When that rate of steward's mate first class went up, heads all around were raised and eyes opened with amazement. No one openly questioned me, and for a while, I was treated much the same. For this, I was thankful. For a while, I didn't mind that my secret was out, but then I didn't know what lay ahead.

Living a lie is bad because it has a peculiar way of showing itself at the most inopportune time. So it was in my case.

I think back now and wonder at the embarrassment of the posting of that rate. There was Miss Rulkey, the head nurse, who classed me as the ward joker and never failed to stop and talk with me. Not so after the rate was out, she rushed past me in a hurry. "Busy," "Be back later," but she never returned.

The knock rummy game that never started without me was now suddenly "too many." It even spread to the Red Cross hut, and finally I just gave up and faked sleep in my bunk.

It seems there was a marine in my ward, and to this day, I don't know his identity. This particular marine was originally from Brighton and, at one time or another, had known Alice, Mary's oldest sister and my future sister-in-law. No doubt he thought he was doing an honorable thing and—being the nosy, helpful person that he was—lost no time in making a special trip to Brighton to tell Alice the whole story. He had seen Mary visiting me and knew she was Alice's sister, and I guess he felt it was his duty to tell Alice that her sister was going with a "White" Negro.

My first knowledge was that the family knew about my fifth week at Chelsea. It was a Sunday, visiting day, and I had been expecting Mary at any moment for the past "hour." She was late, and my first sight of her, she told me that something was wrong. You guessed it—the Marine told Alice, she told the family, and all hell broke loose on Mary. She told me everything, and it wasn't a pretty story. The family had started in on her Saturday morning, and they had kept the argument going Saturday night and all day Sunday.

Mary had fought them with everything she had, but in the end, she had been forbidden ever to see me again. She had not made any promises, but for the sake of peace, she quit arguing. Her silence had been taken by the family to mean that she would comply with their wishes. I listened to the whole story without saying a word, and when she had finished, I still said nothing. I just sat there watching her. I knew how bad the argument had been because it showed in her face. Her eyes were red, swollen, and her face was drawn, probably from a night spent crying with no sleep.

I knew also that she hadn't told me everything. In her own beautiful way, she tried to spare my feelings from those stinging words she had taken so bravely. Words that, if I knew Pop, had been "that God damned nigger," "the no-good bastard," "the cheap Black Protestant," and a lot more that's not worth repeating. She hadn't told me these things, but I knew them just the same.

When at last I did speak, all I could say was "I'm sorry, Mary." Although it wasn't my doing, I still felt the responsibility because I knew just how much trouble my racial lie could cause. I loved Mary more than ever for the stand she had taken, but I knew she was no match for it. This thing, this racial argument, had licked people far greater and bigger than either of us. I knew I had been able to live as I had only through sheer luck and the help of God. This, on top of everything else, was the payoff. I was through, ready to throw in the towel. And then words came free and clear from my lips, and I found myself speaking my innermost thoughts.

I was tired of living a lie, tired of fighting a world filled with hate. Someday maybe there will be free men, equal men, but someone else would fight for it, not me. I was tired of the whole thing, and even if it meant losing her, I still couldn't do anything. We might as well face it—what we wanted could never be. I don't think it even exists; what we had was a fool's dream. I was sick of knocking my head against a steel door that wouldn't open. I suddenly thought of the old adage about "east is east and west is west, and never the twain shall meet." So it is that a Negro is a Negro and a White man is White, and never the two shall meet on equal ground.

I was telling Mary all this; and the more I talked, the madder I got until, at last, I just ran out of words. For a while, we just sat there, and then Mary spoke—a Mary that I had never heard, with a voice as soft as falling snow yet was as cold and as sharp as ice. She laced into me with everything she had, and I couldn't stop her because it was true, every word of it.

With a face that showed no emotion, she started in, "So you're ready to quit, to give up, but what about me? What about all of our plans, our dreams? I was willing to fight the world for you if need be, even to give up my family, and yet at the first sign of trouble, which we expected, you're ready to throw in the towel, as you put it. That's not like you, Bill. To hear you talk, our feelings don't matter at all. Is all this racial trouble more important than we, than our love? You're letting this fear, this hate, or whatever it is become an obsession with you, a constant barrier between us. In a way, I guess it is, but refuse to let it wreck our lives."

She was beginning to cry but still went on. "I'm twenty-one, Bill, and I love you, love you, more than anything else in the world. And I don't want to lose you. Can't you see that if you continue to let this hatred of racial prejudice come between us, then you are helping it to lick you. If you can't, I can. I can see it making me lose the one thing on earth I want most—you. I've told you before that nothing can ever change my love for you."

She was crying freely now, and as I sat there, I could feel myself breaking. Yes, I could feel the hot sting of tears in my own eyes, and it was all I could do to hold them back. She was true blue and clear through, and as I held her there in my arms, I knew that racial trouble would never come between us again. Someday, some way, we would lick it together. Say what you may, but with a girl like that, how could I lose? We were young and in love, and there was a life-time before us to fight for. I remembered the old saying that anything new or worth fighting for never came quickly or easily. It would be slow and hard, and I must face it as such.

How many times have we excused mistakes or faults to the folly of youth, and yet isn't youth one of the greatest gifts to mankind? It creates ideals, makes crusaders, and, best of all, it keeps an old world vibrant, full of life, and continually living through sorrow, happiness, war, peace, and all the other thousand and one manifestations of man's mind. Mistakes we make through youth, yes, but not to make them comes only with age and experience. For that reason, few of us would change it if we could. Thank God, this love between Mary and me was not a mistake of youth but, as time proved, a youth's dream fulfilled.

I had entered the hospital to be cured of a stomach disorder and was quite surprised when at the end of six weeks, I was informed there's no cure. It seemed I was unfit for sea duty and with a nervous stomach to boot. It was decided I would be given a medical discharge. My trouble would cure itself in one, maybe two years, on the outside; to anyone who was in the service, three and a half years. There is no need to tell you "I wanted out."

It's strange how sometimes the solving of one problem merely opens the door for a number of others to come in. I now had a new life to make, new job, new friends, and a strange new city to live in. There was still the trouble with Mary's family and still the problem of settling down and making a success of my life for Mary's sake, and this I had to do.

A week before my discharge, I bought all-new civilian clothes and was settled in a cute two-room apartment in Brookline that Mary had found for me. Everything was perfect; I was fast getting acclimated to civilian life with only one important thing left—to get a job. This wasn't too much of a problem except that I didn't know what I really wanted to do. I could always go back to cooking or cabinetmaking, but I kept thinking of sales work. I made a decision about two weeks after my discharge, or rather Mary did.

It was a bright sunny Saturday morning, and we were meeting in town for breakfast and to spend the day together. The moment I saw her, I knew she was excited about something; and like a kid with a "deep dark secret," she kept me in suspense until we were comfortably seated, and breakfast ordered. She fairly bubbled over with joy as she shoved an ad section of one of the local newspapers in front of me. I still didn't get it, but I started reading a business for sale that she had circled so carefully.

"A going delicatessen café business would like a working partner with some food and business know-how. Good chance for right party. Phone so-and-so number for appointment."

Laying the paper down and taking a sip of coffee, I asked Mary, "Would you mind explaining just what this is all about?"

Her answer was one of complete innocence as though I should have known everything from reading the ad. In her own words, "It is quite simple. I know the place. It is a shopping center in my own neighborhood, a good little business with maybe a few modern improvements needed, and it is perfect for you."

When I didn't answer for a while, she asked, "What's the matter? Don't you think it's a good idea?"

I looked at her, and restraining myself from laughing the best way I know how, I answered, "Darling, you sweet innocent thing, it's wonderful except for one little thing. The ad says a small amount of capital, and if the business is any good, that means about three times the small amount I have. And furthermore, what I have, I'm keeping to marry the most wonderful girl in the world, understand?"

This didn't satisfy her, and she kept plugging away. She knew I had $3,600 to the round figure in the bank and, with her $800, would make a total of $4400; and that might swing it. I told her it was no-go for a number of reasons, and one above all was that I wouldn't touch her money—in marriage, yes, but before, no. We argued pro and con all through breakfast and on my third cup of coffee with points in her favor such as we could get married sooner, I could get set in business, and it would show her family we could get along. I reluctantly agreed to call him.

In a shy, childlike way, Mary asked, "You wouldn't mind seeing him this afternoon would you, Bill? Say, about two o'clock?"

Seeing she was still hiding something, I said, "Why this afternoon? I've got to call him first, or don't I?"

"Don't be mad, Bill, but I have already called him and made the appointment for two o'clock."

I couldn't be angry with her; I just sat there half smiling, looking at her, and finally said, "Remind me to break that beautiful neck of yours after we're married. In the meantime, let's get ready to see about this big business deal that I don't, for the life of me, know how I got mixed up in."

At this we both broke—into laughter.

As they say, "It's never the big things that change our lives. It's the small, inconsequential happenings that so often we forget." A big change takes place; but we can't put our finger on the exact why, when, or where of its beginning. That's how it was with me. My big chance had started, but I didn't know it. That small ad and a carefree breakfast had really been the beginning.

Two o'clock found us in front of "Harry's Delicatessen," an unimposing little place that had once been a shoe store and then converted into café. The inside furnishings included a greasy linoleum counter and stools that had lived ten years too long and four wooden tables, well worn with use and cigarette burns. There were a half dozen people in the place eating sandwiches, a young girl waiting on customers, and, behind the counter, a five-and-a-half-feet-tall butterball of a guy chopping onions that I guessed was the owner of this "going business."

I spoke to him and said I was there in reference to the ad.

He sized me up with that look you generally give a woman—you know the kind, look her up and down and then right through her—nodded his head, and said, "Be with you in a minute. Sit down and have a cup of coffee."

I have to admit the more I saw of the place, the less I liked it. When he had finished crying over the onions, he drew a cup of coffee and came over and sat down. I introduced Mary and myself and shook hands while he told me he was Harry Cohen, the owner of, as he put it, "this delicatessen that should be making money hand over fist but was barely breaking even."

Harry didn't pull any punches; he was downright honest from the beginning. He had come out of the service, married, and sunk every cent he had in the place but, for one reason or another, just hadn't been able to make it click. Two months ago, he had gotten the idea to remodel the place—modernize it, so to speak. Cutting all expenses to the bone, it would take about $3,500; and for that much cash, he would give a man a half working interest in everything. Basically, it was as simple as that. They were doing an average business, but I would be buying into a fast-folding business. In other words, without a doubt, a $3,500 gamble.

We talked for about an hour while he jumped up now and then to make sandwiches. By the time we left, I knew everything about Harry, and he knew practically all about me. I say "practically all" because I didn't mention my race. I just said I was from Texas. I told Harry I had the money and was a cook but that I would like a few days to think it over. He had a couple of other people in to see about it—one didn't have quite enough money and the other Harry just plain didn't like. So I figured nothing would happen for a few days. Mary was completely sold on the idea. I wasn't. But I knew I had to start somewhere, and this looked like as good a chance as any.

Four days later, I went back to see Harry with a proposition to make to him. I would buy provided we stayed open from 6:00 a.m. to midnight (they now close at 8:00 p.m.) with me working the second shift. My idea here was to try to get the young trade around the center at night and to catch the movie turnout. Install juke box and new counter and tables. Some of the carpentry work and painting, I could do myself to save on labor cost. If he was agreeable to this, I would buy in. We could get lawyers and draw up papers that night. I didn't know it then, but Harry was against the wall, and that $3,500 was the answer to everything.

He was as honest as they come and a hard worker. When I look back now to the long hours and hard work we both put in, I see why we succeeded. It wasn't as easy as I have made it sound here. To give you an example, it was two years of untold hard work and worry before we really had it good and were able to take it easy. That first year—oh, brother—how I wished time and time again that I had never bought in. But in I was, and there was nothing else to do but make the place pay. Without my hard work and money, Harry would have been out; and without his hard work and business know-how, we could have never made it pay. But together we did. We ran the place six years, the last four of which were real moneymakers for us. The business mushroomed into a gold mine, and six years and four months from the date I bought in, we sold out at a beautiful price. In that time, there had been heated arguments and differences of opinion, but Harry and I became very close friends and are still to this day. Harry is in business again, doing well, and I bought a place outside of town on a well-traveled highway. Mary and I ran it together with the help of a cook and one waitress.

Harry and I have talked about opening a café in Downtown Boston, and considering we made it together, who knows someday maybe we'll go broke together. Such is life.

This all seems so long ago now, but in reality, it hasn't been. Mary and I have come a long way since then but not without a hard fight. We've fought every inch of the way and, to be truthful, enjoyed every minute of it. You know why? Because we're winning the battle, and someday we will lick it.

Oh yes, I'd almost forgotten; there were still Pops and Mary's family—my future in-laws. We settled that in an easy way. Just let nature take its course, or better still, "Let a sleeping dog lie." We had postponed our marriage because of business, and for Mary's sake, I still wanted her family's friendship and blessing.

Pop knew Mary was seeing me every day, and for a while, there was an argument every time. She left the house, but when everyone saw how well we were doing, they gave in completely. We were married; and afterward, thanks to Pop, there was a big reception.

Pop and everyone had changed. They were accepting me on my own merit, not on my race or religion but as a free human being. Today, as I said before, I couldn't ask for better in-laws.

I have never regretted my marriage, and I pray that Mary shall never have cause to. We have been married eight years now and have a lovely tow-headed girl, Carol Ann, aged six. We are as happy and as much in love as any two people God ever made and from all outlooks. I think it will grow sweeter as we go through the years together. It's a tough road to travel, but we think it's worthwhile. To those of you who attempt to travel it, always remember that somehow, right will win out and that you need true friends and faith above all else. As Woodrow Wilson once said, "Friendship is the only cement that will ever hold the world together."

In one sense, this is true; but on the other hand, I would like to add faith—faith in each other and in our fellow man, faith in our country and our world, and faith in the new generation to come. Some of you will ask, "What is faith?" A complete definition of the word, as I understand it, is something that you cannot see or feel, an intangible, that comes into being through an inner feeling of belief. Today, the world stands on the threshold of an unpredictable new era. Once more, as in all times of trial, we Americans and the world are turning to faith as a steadfast guide in the search for security, comfort, and peace of mind during the days to come. Confidence and hope have weakened and waned under the weight of problems which beset the globe and its people. Deeply troubled for the future, man seeks new directions, and modern times have isolated him as never before. In an age of astounding technological maturity, many of the rich values of the past have been lost or forgotten. Too often each of us walks alone. Yet there are many in this land whose faces are an unclouded reflection of inner confidence which draws on the eternal well of faith. Their eyes look forward without fear.

There are pathways leading toward the ever-renewed hope that our children and our children's children will inherit a world awakened to the possibility of unity and peace. To achieve this, children must grow up in the aura of a familiar faith and receive from their elders the direction and guidance that lie in the words of wisdom. These teachings can never fade or change.

In the days of our greatest happiness or in the disturbing times of tribulation and distress, faith constantly guides our hand and governs our heart. For man knows that the difficulties of life are less trying when he can look forward always with serenity and without fear. In this way, the future can be faced with courage, and there is a composure and an inner light which sheds its rays on the peaceful succeeding day. With these things—faith, confidence, and hope—though his search may be endless, he will never be alone.

For then, security and peace of mind prevail and govern the years of his life and the lives of all mankind. Yes, I believe that faith can and will hold the world together. Even the basic secret of the Christian religion is not effort or willpower, important as they are; the secret is faith. When we have learned to have faith, we become a channel for the flow of divine power.

VIII

Since starting to write this book, a lot of important things have happened concerning racial intolerance and religious hatred. One such thing on which I touched lightly elsewhere in this book was the Supreme Court's decision on integration in May 1954. The day this bill was passed has become more commonly called "Black Monday" throughout the South.

Councils, clubs, and groups have banded together to fight integration and defy the federal government. The question in my mind is: Are the councils incipient Ku Klux Klan? If not, can they or will they come in time to resemble the later-day Klan of hideous memory?

These citizens' councils or groups, which so far have spread unchecked into almost every Southern State, can become instruments of interracial violence. The ingredients are there; the spark is lacking so far. If and when that should appear, I warn and predict that the men in white robes or burners will seize control.

There have been some shocking stories come out of the South in relation to integration. Some are humorous on the one hand and sad and pathetic on the other.

In Mississippi, prizes are being offered to school children for a review of the booklet *Black Monday: The Day of the Supreme Court's Decision* written by a Mississippi circuit judge. Its thesis is that a single-school system means "mongrelization." It says the people of Italy, Greece, Spain, and the South American countries are decadent because of admixture with the Negro and lays the fall of ancient civilization to Negro integration.

Alabama state senator Walter C. Givhan won front-page notoriety when he charged that the ultimate goal of the NAACP was to open the bedroom doors of their White women to Negro men. Givhan also foresees the election of a Negro vice president and the eventual assassination of the White president by Negroes so that a Negroid dynasty can take over.

Another incident that integration brought about was the humorous proclamation issued by the then governor of Georgia against Georgia Tech students playing football against Pittsburgh in the Sugar Bowl because of a Negro player on the Pittsburgh team. I say humorous because the very students he was trying to protect rioted and hung his honor, Governor Marvin Griffin, in effigy.

This was a bad move on Governor Griffin's part that backfired on him, and well, it should. As I said before, I believe the younger generation on would forget this racial fight and accept integration completely if the older generation would let them.

In the dark words of the hillbilly statesman from the grits-and-hominy state, it is unlawful, a disgrace, and sinful when White boys indulge in tests of athletic skill with Black boys and Colored America sit with White America side by side in the stand.

It looks like the governor, in the interest of statesmanship, will have to drop a cotton curtain around Georgia, smash all television and radio sets, prohibit the import of out-of-state newspapers, and burn a lot of books, including the Bible.

If Governor Griffin and others like him in the South had their way, the voice of Marian Anderson would have been lost in loneliness; and Dr. George Washington Carver would not have synthetic marble, wood shavings, ink-insulating board, and a hundred other products from the common everyday peanut or rubber from the sweet potato. If their unprincipled principles had prevailed, Georgia Tech students would not have rebelled against their leader. Thank God, these principles are dying slow and hard, but they are dying.

On another occasion, a Mississippi Negro schoolteacher joined the Roman Catholic and began attending service in a White Catholic Church without hindrance, as happens in many Catholic churches in the South. She lost her job.

So the stories continue to run, unendingly, all over the South. I have no way to check or know how many are true or how many have council or club members as protagonists. The main thing is that Mississippi, Alabama, and Georgia Negroes believe them and so do many Southern White, some approvingly and others with disgust and pity.

Stupid? Yes. Crackpots? No. These are the people and thoughts that make for a Ku Klux Klan, a Hitler, and another war. I am certain that should a provocative incident result in violent reaction, the decent citizens will desert the councils today just as they did yesterday's Ku Klux Klan. Unfortunately, the desertion would not be the death of the hooded riders. It would only mean that the hoodlums and the ignorant would gain control. That is the greatest danger.

The one difference, which is the hopeful one between today and the white robes of yesterday riders, is that the federal government will not tolerate, as it did a generation ago, lawlessness that definitely violates Bill of Rights and the Constitution.

I cannot imagine the federal government failing to intervene harshly in any widespread, organized, and racially-motivated terrorism.

The mob which in years gone by would hang its victims to the nearest tree or tie the hapless Negro to the stake for public burning is now about obsolete, thanks to years of effort by the NAACP and an aroused America. Instead, the old-style public lynching has been replaced by bombings, beatings, and killings by three or four persons rather than by a mob of thousands. Also, economic pressure, the denial of jobs, and the withholding of credit from Negro homeowners, farmers, and business and professional men have been used increasingly to replace the cruder, bloodier forms of intimidation and terror.

Fate, God, history, and external and internal pressures—take your choice—led the Supreme Court of the United States to declare that racially separate school facilities, no matter how equal, are discriminatory and unconstitutional. But neither God nor man devised a way to make unconvinced people accept such a verdict immediately as wise or practical to themselves.

I don't like the councils. That is not to say that I am blind to the tears that prompt them or to the dilemma of the South today. What I am sure of is that the councils' way is not the right way. It is not American to say that unless you are with me, you are an enemy. It is not American to bully the defenseless and the minority of dissenters. It is not American to deprive or seek to deprive any group of their freedom or their rights. It is not American to invoke the doctrine that there is a master race or superrace as Hitler tried to do.

This is ready-made trouble for all minorities. I ask everyone reading this always to remember that the world has time and again been plunged into darkness and with the seemingly small acts against a small minority by a group or council such as these.

Red China versus Nationalist China and Korea, Hitler versus Poland and the Jews, Mussolini versus Ethiopia—the list is endless.

Think, remember, and then act accordingly. Your religion, your race, or your way of life could be next.

These councils or groups, whatever their aim or ultimate goal be, are spawned in the fertile swamps of prejudice, hate, and ignorance.

Freedom has been the click word of every generation of the human race since the world began. It has sparked every revolution the world has ever seen. Each generation desires to be free from the conventions which bound its predecessors and instinctively tries to throw off the shackles of all restraint.

With the eyes of the world upon America for democratic leadership, the task ahead is gigantic. The United States must prove her sincerity to those who mistrust this country because of mistreatment of minority groups. Every vestige of race bigotry and segregation must be quickly eliminated from American life. The time to begin this preparation is now. The place to begin is within one's own heart, one's own house. The law against segregation has been passed by the highest court in the land; and the sooner we, as good citizens, obey the law, the better. The South has able leaders who can solve these problems—if they want to and really try to.

Our forefathers started this great nation of ours with beautiful, idealistic visions of freedom and equality for all, but by the time the idea emerged that everyone in a democracy should be educated, prejudice had induced so many reservations that the word "everyone" had taken on a new, small, and awful meaning.

"Everyone should be educated, but of course, not the Negroes."

"Everyone should be educated, but not too many Jews."

"Everyone should be educated—that is, everyone except women."

These things are somewhat changed today but not completely.

Prejudice is still insisting that education be withheld from some people because their race, religion, or national origin is alien to that group or council in power.

Where a Jew is doomed to an inferior or inexpedient education, "we have entered upon a process that leads to a spiritual and intellectual degradation hardly less terrifying than the gas chambers of Buchenwald."

When the Negro, in a land that he considers the Motherland, is denied an equal opportunity to secure an education in order to be of great service to his community and his nation, we have entered upon a process of intellectual demoralization hardly less barbaric than the rope and club of the hooded night rider.

I hope and pray that as we move into a new stage in the battle against ignorance and the struggle for peace and freedom of the world, all men's minds are freed from the impediments of suspicion and superstition and of racial and religious intolerance.

I have crossed over the invisible barred line of race and color, the color barrier, but I have not deserted my people. I will continue to love and help them with a deep understanding born oppression. I will continue to do all in my power to help their cause. I pray that morality and right are with me.

It is indeed sad when either a man or a nation has a perfectly moral job to do but somehow fails to explain other to himself or to the world why the task is important and upon what moral principles it is based.

I can only hope that this book explains all these things and more. I say to you again. I was never ashamed of my race, the Negro. My crossing the color line was a simple homespun fact; I wanted a better way of life. I wanted freedom from hate, tyranny, prejudice, and the thousand and one other sins that man perpetrates against man, especially the Negro race, in the name of law and right. I was successful. I help my body to escape, but I know now that my soul and my mind will never be free.

I will never be able to read of a prejudice hate against any race without my heart bleeding for that race and its people. Sometimes after reading of a race riot or the persecution of some religious group, my soul cries out against the inhumanity of it all. I have prayed that God would show mankind the way out of his darkness and help guide our feet back to the path of righteousness.

Man will someday realize that we are "all God's children," and one day, the oppressor and the oppressed shall stand before Him in judgment. Side by side, we will stand and equally be tried.

There will be but one religion there, the love of God. There will be but one race, the children of God, brothers and sisters all. There will be but one country, the kingdom of God. With these inescapable facts before us, man is indeed a fool. All this fighting on earth is such a senseless battle.

"Pray ye. Forgive us, Father, as we forgive ours."

IX

A serious problem in my life and one facing the human race in the world today is this matter called "miscegenation," by which is meant marriage outside of one's kind. Specifically, here in America, miscegenation refers to the marriage of Colored and Whites. In reality, miscegenation is an anthropological process which has been going on since the beginning of time. In many states of this country, marriages are illegal if the parties to it are not of the same color. This applies not only to Negroes but to the Indian, Mexican, Chinese, and other races. To me it is impossible to say not the same race because so little is known of the races of a man although in Hitler's time, the radical theories of Houston, Stewart, Chamberlain, and others like them were emphasized for political purposes. Yet no one could regard the Germans as a "pure race," for they have been invaded so often by so many varieties of man. Similarly, it would be difficult to ignore the role of the Moors in Southern Europe and the mixed relationships among the Romans, the Goths, the Vandals, Hannibal's armies— need one go on?

Of course, moral law can recognize no such rule of life even though all men and women are God's children. In the earlier history of European civilization, national or racial differences were rarely recognized. The Greek and Roman conquerors took their women where they found them, and although concubinage may not always have produced legitimate offspring, the descendants of such unions influenced the general character of the European population. Similarly, all through Asia and in North Africa, the mixtures of man have been continuous.

Asiatic women have generally held a fascination for Western man. They are so mild and generous, and when they are beautiful, they are without compare. And one needs only to be married into a Chinese family to discover that women as wives are universally patterned and that beneath the pigmentation of the skin is a woman, wife, and a mother.

I can only throw my mind back to my own lovely wife and to the days when we discussed our own racial differences as a practical problem that we had to solve, just as it faces in this world today. We did solve it firmly and practically to our satisfaction. And at no time, so far as I know, have there been any regrets or uncertainties. We are a husband and wife racing through life together, and our problems are never personal.

Certainly, there must be miscegenation of a horrible kind in a count that produces so much divorce and often so early in a marriage. What happiness can there be in a marriage of the same kind of people that smashes upon the rocks of incompatibility which can only mean selfishness and egocentricity—so soon after marriage that the normal adjustments of human being to human being, of personality to personality, could not yet have taken place.

And how difficult it is for one who has been happily married to understand this movement of a good woman from husband to husband, from one man to another, time after time.

This is nothing to push aside as a hateful subject not to be discussed but rather one that we must face openly, a subject that every human being is responsible for.

My marriage or miscegenational union, whichever you prefer to call it, has been filled with problems—problems that are as much the public's as our own and problems that we worked long and hard to solve.

To give you a better picture, I will list the more important problems of a mixed marriage in a question-and-answer series, but before doing, so I should like to explain that these answers refer to *our* marriage.

They may or may not conform to the standards of the public, the church, or the world. They are decisions and plans we have used in our marriage and are using now.

Believing I know a little of human nature I will answer the foremost and most important question that is in everyone's mind at first.

Q. How did we plan to meet the situation had our daughter borne Negro characteristics, or had we never faced such a situation?

A. This is one of the greatest worries of one who has crossed the color line or passing. One school of thought says it is a myth, an old maids' tale. It's the old story of the "throwback," the chance of a tar-black baby when either parent has even a drop of Negro blood. Anthropologists and biologists call it an impossibility when both parties to the marriage are White skinned. They say the pigmentation of all races is in the outer skin, and the true under akin is the same color in all human beings.

I must admit that the only truthful answer I can give is that we solved it with hope and prayer. By this, I mean that we had talked the problem over together and knew there was no surefire method of avoiding it. It was a definite threat to the success of my new life and marriage. I am no doctor but will explain another school of thought from the slight medical fact I know on the subject, the same as I explained to Mary. First, the problem of color, hair, features, and other hereditary factors.

To begin with, heredity only goes back three generations to decide these things. This makes for fourteen people, including the parents on both sides, to decide these questions.

On Mary's side, there was no such worry. Her family on both her mother's and father's side had been White skinned through generation after generation. That much was in our favor. The odds were further narrowed on my family's side due to the fact that my mother, grandmother, and great-grandmother had been light skinned with no Negro characteristics. This left the immovable fact of the dark color and characteristics of my father's family tree.

From a gambling point of view, the odds were on our side for White-skinned children with White characteristics, and there was nothing to do but pray and hope.

I realize that other mixed marriages may not or have not been so successful and lucky as ours. To these unfortunates, I am truly sorry that I have no answer.

Some people feel and believe that regardless of children, mixed marriages will solve the racial antagonism question. I truthfully don't know. It may help in making the public accept mixed marriages. It probably will help racial relationship, but—and this is the main thing—it has first to be approved and accepted by the public.

This is a problem that does not end with the birth of a White-skinned child to the mixed marriage couple. It continues all through a child's life. In our case, and maybe we are wrong, we never intend to tell our daughter. We own property in a White neighborhood.

I live and work as a White, attend a White church, and, to all outward appearances, there never need be any show or mention of my Negro birth.

Some of you will say I am living a lie and helping my children to live a lie. To you, I say that I am not because I am White in color. *I am a White man.*

Unfortunately, due to circumstances, my daughter will never be able to see her grandparents on my side, and that presents no problem luckily because my mother and father live so far away.

In other words, inwardly I may feel and fight tor the Negro; but outwardly, in reference to my private life, I have divorced the Negro race completely.

Q. What do I feel I have accomplished by my "going over" other than the personal satisfaction of proving a Negro is as good as a White man?

A. To begin with, when I crossed over, it was not to prove a point but to gain a better way of life; and this, I feel, I have done.

Proving Negro is as good as a White man needs to be done only for the ignorant. A man is a man first, regardless of his color, and we find the same types and kinds in all races.

I do feel I have been, and am making, a social contribution to the problems of racial understanding. I belong to the NAACP and work whenever possible in the interest of the Negroes' problems so long as it doesn't jeopardize my family's happiness. I also belong to the YMCA, the PTA, and the local Red Cross unit and am an active working member. These four important organizations take up all my spare time, and I firmly believe they are all important to my family and city.

As far as being successful in life, I think I have accomplished that. Success comes easy in this country, twice as easy to a White man. There are many ways to make money, and they all spell success.

We measure greatness by the distance between the dream and the failure. We all fail. None of us ever matches the dream, but as an average working American, I feel I have been very successful.

Q. How did my wife come to be so broad minded as to accept me racially and religiously, and how has her family accepted our marriage?

A. My wife's accepting, I believe, was done basically because of her racial ignorance. By this, I mean her mind had never been touched by the problem, the age-old fight of racial hatred. She had been born and reared in a Catholic family in a White neighborhood with no real outside contact with the Negro. As such, when we meet, she fell in love with me for myself as a man and not my racial background.

As to religion, we were, as most young people today, broad minded on the subject. She is a Catholic, and I am a Protestant, Baptist. And we both still are. She attends the church of her choice and I of mine, and this I feel has never been or ever will be a problem to our racial intermarriage. Our daughter is being raised as a Catholic.

As to her family's feelings, I am afraid we will never truthfully know. You must understand for reputation in the neighborhood, they were forced to accept me because, I guess you would say, this has all been a dark family secret known only to the family and few intimate friends.

I must admit though; I do believe they have accepted me completely. There have never been any outward signs or indications that they don't. On the whole, I can truthfully say I get along with them far better than the average son-in-law relationship does.

Q. What is the relationship between me and my parents at the present time and in the future?

A. Wonderful.

There exists between us the same love, devotion, and family ties that exist between any mother, father, and son.

There are some problems that I know will never be solved, but they know and understand all about my marriage and help us in any way they can. Their first concern, as all mothers and fathers have, is the happiness of their child—in this case, their son and his family. I get home at least once a year to visit. Mary has been down twice, and my mother has been to visit us once. Needless to say, on these visits, when Mary and my family met, it was necessary to meet in a distant city, a few miles from each of our own home cities.

These are but a few of the untold thousands of problems that show themselves in a mixed marriage. I could not begin to answer all of them here because that in itself would be a book. I have tried, as best I could in a layman's language, to answer some or the more prominent and important ones as they affected us and our marriage.

There are a few other questions that do not concern my marriage directly, but I feel I should give an answer to them here.

Q. Will integration mean any difference to me or my family? Will I make any change?

A. Integration will mean as much to me and my family as it will to millions of other with a sense of decency in their hearts and to see a wrong made right. Among other things, it will mean a greater and more humble respect for this great nation of ours.

As for me or my family making any changes, the answer is no. I will feel and be thankful for the great victory won by my people, the Negro. I will be proud for any little part I may have played to bring about the victory, but that is all.

My life now is such that it is more than just myself to be considered. There's my wife, my children, my business associates, my friends, and so much more to be thought of. I cannot make any changes because I entered upon a one-way road that I am too far down to turn around and come back. I don't know if I would want to, even if I could.

Q. Some of you ask, "Will the South accept integration? Do I believe it will succeed in the South without bloodshed, and if so, how long before it will be accepted as everyday life?

A. The law makes integration mandatory, but it does not ensure its successful acceptance. That comes from the public with the exception of a few hotheads, the old die-hard rebels, and ignorant, poverty-stricken Whites. I think the South will accept integration.

As a prophecy, I believe that Texas—which is southwest, not Southern rebel as some believe—will capitulate and back the law of integration to the limit. I believe this because most of Texas is a state of forward-looking men with honesty, integrity, and a strong sense of fair play, decency, and right. I believe that a lot of the Southern States have men of the same high caliber that in time, a short time, will bring about the acceptance of this law and the Negro people.

Integration will succeed in the South definitely, and I give these immovable reasons for it. It had been made the law of the country by the highest court in the land, the Supreme Court, and will be so enforced by the federal government.

As to its success without bloodshed, all I can do is to say a fervent prayer against it. I think there will be some scattered incidents but no more than what is usual in the South. Remember, there were three cold-blooded Negro murders in Mississippi due to racial troubles in 1955.

Q. Isn't this book an open admission that integration means intermarriage and that the Negro wants it?

A. No, it is not. This book is "my" life and not that of the Negro people. I intermarried, but I did not change over for that purpose. Marriage came later. The Negro doesn't want intermarriage any more than the White man does. His want for integration involves things far more important than that. I will give two examples here that are simple and to the point.

One night recently, a friend and I went to the fights at the arena in Boston. The seat prices were $7.00, $5.00, $2.75, and $1.25. We bought two $5 seats that were good seats with an unobstructed view, and we enjoyed the fight. Just ahead of us, at ringside, I noticed two Negroes sitting in $7 seats. They were sitting in front of over six thousand people. They had paid to sit there because they wanted to see the fight close-up instead of half a block away in what we cruelly call Nigger Heaven.

Every person in that Arena had the equal chance and right to sit where he or she pleased or where his pocketbook would let him. His ability to pay decided his place to sit, not his race, his color, or his religion; and that is as it should be. Not so in the South though. Good seats are vacant at the theatres, fights, circuses, concerts, and other public gatherings; and Negroes, regardless of their rights, desires, or ability to pay, are relegated to the last ten or fifteen seats in the balcony in the rear.

Franklin Delano Roosevelt visited our town when I was just a child, and like every other child, my father took me to see him. He was to make a speech in a public park. Seats were set up for Whites, but the Negro population couldn't enter a White park and was given permission to stand outside in the street. I remember my father hoisting me high on his shoulder to try to see over that sea of heads for one glimpse of the president of the United States. I saw him, if you can class a blurred head movement a block away as seeing. On the other hand—let's face it—I wouldn't have recognized him from that one view if that night he had come into my own home.

Integration means the end of all discriminatory acts of this kind. The Negro will be free to enjoy equally all the benefits that the Whites enjoy in work and play. The Negro's dollar will then buy the same as the White man's in culture, art, and education. His standard of living will be raised. He will live in better homes, and he will be a better citizen to his neighborhood, his state, and his country.

These are just a few of the things that integration means to the Negro. Intermarriage certainly is not one of the wants of the Negro people. To begin with, intermarriage isn't planned; it just happens.

These are questions and answers, my thoughts, and my beliefs that only time will give a true answer to. They are problems that every American will have to help solve.

Negroes and Whites alike must remember that since the beginning of time, man has fought most progress and all changes. Why? Because man is afraid of change. He is a creature of habit; and as such, he clings to the old and the tried and true and is afraid of change because he doesn't understand it. He is afraid of a future that he can't see or comprehend. He fought new thoughts of science, new ideas of medicine, new government, and any religion different from his own because he didn't understand them. Thank God there has been and always will be men of vision, foresight, and integrity to bring about these changes. Remember when the automobile never would replace the horse and buggy, man was not made to fly like a bird, and I am sure that most of us can remember when any reference to a spaceship was made, we laughed and immediately thought of some nut drawing or comic strip.

These things were all fought as any change is, but they came to be and were accepted nevertheless.

As such, I know that the barrier against integration and the Negro will came to pass, melt, and disappear as all barriers against change have done in the past. They must if this nation is to survive and continue to hold its Constitution and Bill of Rights up for all the world to see. We must if we are to prove to other nations that ours is indeed the land of the "free" and the home of the "brave." We must because the eyes of the world are upon us.

As I have said before, I am only a small man in a large world, and I intend to remain that way. I am not famous, nor do I expect to achieve fame. This book was written only for the purpose of trying to help right a wrong and to expose a grave injustice that feeds on the world of today. I have not tried to glorify my life or the facts thereof. These are minor everyday happenings that unfold a thousand times a day on the stage of life.

I have not told tales of violence and terror in this book mainly because I have not seen a lot of it. Yes, I've heard stories, gossip, and old maids' tales. Some are true, no doubt, and some false; but I can't swear to their authenticity. Under these conditions, I prefer to say as little as possible about them.

In closing this section of my life, I would like to leave you with the proverb by John Stuart Mills: "The only freedom which deserves the name is that of pursuing our own good in our own way, so long as we do not attempt to deprive others of theirs or impede their efforts to obtain it."

This is indeed food for thought because millions of decent Americans have long forgotten the basics truth—that every human being receives his fundamental rights from God, not as we are being led to believe, from the state or government. Our Declaration of Independence repeatedly tells us to protect those God-given rights. For most of us to believe that these rights are safe today is pure folly, a fool's dream. You ask, How can you or I remedy this and better condition for our fellow man? To you, I say, "Willingness without action is like a cloud without rain. There may be lots of thunder and lightning, but no parched ground is watered." Remember first that all people and races of the world want to be truly loved, not just tolerated. Always try to see their better side instead of using their bad faults against them. In being realistic, we do not always have to be pessimistic. Christ never blinked his eyes at bad things, but he never became so obsessed with human evil that he lost faith in man. Quit going through life "with the crowd."

By that, I mean express your thoughts and convictions no matter how the "crowd" feels. We all have *good* in us, and some of you reading this agree with me except that you are shy and timid and are ashamed to express yourselves and to exert your rights. You will never contribute much to the world, your race, or the new generation as long as you wait for others to lead the way. Abraham Lincoln said on the day of his nomination, "Let us pray God and forget all this quibbling, about these men and that man, about this race and that race. Let us all unite and let men look out over this great nation of ours with all free men equal." We could all practice this today.

It's up to you to become a leader yourself and find friendship and happiness among your fellowmen. Pave the way so that the future generations, the world over, may live in closer harmony.

Keep in mind that your children and my children's children are depending on us, on you, and on everyone reading this book to be a guiding hand to make a better world for them.

There is a poem written about our children by Rajat Chaubham which reads:

> Your children are not your children.
> They are the sons and daughters of life's
> longing for itself,

They come through you but not from you,
And though they are with you they belong
not to you:
You may give them your love but not your
thoughts
For they have their own thoughts.
You may house their bodies but not their souls
For their souls' dwell in the house of tomorrow
Which you cannot visit, not even in your
dreams.
You may strive to be like them
But seek not to make them like you
For life goes not backward, nor tarries
with yesterday.

Make a world better than the one we now live on, one that gives them the freedom and rights they so richly deserve and that God intended all humans to have. Let prejudice and hate be lost in the pages of history. These things are in our power. Let's not tail the future generations of the world; and always remember above all else we are—no matter what the race, religion, or color—"all God's children."

As I was writing this book, I think I had the idea inside that maybe this would sort of sum up my life in some way. I realize now that is impossible because I do not know the ending. All I can say is that I feel I am living a good life and a happy one. I have a good home and family. That is not to say that I don't have the pains of memory because I do. Frustrated and mixed up as my childhood was, I did know love and joy, and I loved the Negro people and their way or life. I wanted more from life than the Negro race could hope to get or give me, so I "passed as White" to achieve it. Sometimes when I'm in Boston with time on my hands, I stroll down Huntington Avenue to Massachusetts and Columbus Avenues. I know quite a few people there; so I go down, sit, and have a few drinks. I listen to the laughter of an oppressed but still happy people. I listen to the music, to the Blues and folk songs, sung with deep feeling and understanding from the depths of the heart; and if I let myself think, I become lonesome—lonesome for a way of life and people that I had so long ago but can never have again, not even in my fondest dreams.

I can't turn back. It's too late now.

THE END

About the Author

William "Tex" Pointer was born on August 6, 1923, in Ennis, Texas, to Mozell and Charlie Pointer.

After graduation, he enlisted in the coast guard. He spent time in the navy as a cook. Upon leaving the navy, he changed his life direction. Going forward he would live his life as White and put the Negro life behind him. He took various jobs in Boston, Massachusetts, as a short-order cook. He then moved to New England and married. He had four children. He became a master carpenter and then on to become a machinist. He wrote for numerous newspapers and was also involved in the local politics. Tex enjoyed writing about historical and current events. During his life span, he wrote several books. This was his last book.

Tex eventually passed in 1998 from throat cancer but not before he had touched the lives of numerous individuals. Mary passed away that same year. Their surviving children made the decision to publish his book in 2021.